BETWEEN FIRE AND SLEEP

JAROSLAW ANDERS

Between Fire and Sleep

Essays on Modern Polish Poetry and Prose

YALE UNIVERSITY PRESS · NEW HAVEN AND LONDON

To Anders and Rowan

Published with assistance from the foundation established in memory of Philip Hamilton McMillan of the Class of 1894, Yale College.

Library of Congress Cataloging-in-Publication Data
Anders, Jaroslaw, 1950–
Between fire and sleep: essays on modern Polish poetry and prose / Jaroslaw Anders.
p.   cm.
Includes bibliographical references and index.
ISBN 978-0-300-20746-0 (cloth : alk. paper)
1. Polish literature — 20th century — History and criticism.
I. Title.
PG7051.A53   2009
891.8'5090073 — dc22
2008047083

A catalogue record for this book is available from the British Library.

This paper meets the requirements of ANSI/NISO Z39.48-1992 (Permanence of Paper).
It contains 30 percent postconsumer waste (PCW) and is certified by the Forest Stewardship Council (FSC).

10 9 8 7 6 5 4 3 2 1

CONTENTS

PREFACE

At first, this book may look like a sort of farewell—a long Polish good-bye to a certain way of reading, of living with literature, that was predominant in the Eastern Europe of my youth and that is no more largely owing to the bloodless revolution of 1989, which changed not only the political but also the cultural and moral landscape of my native realm. But we know that Polish good-byes are sham. No one ever leaves before the party is over. Let's say, therefore, that the book is an attempt at a reconstruction of a certain mode of thinking about literature that has shaped my generation (born around the middle of the past century), a mode that often appears strange or even naïve to those who came after us.

This book is also a kind of return—one of those awkward returns of an East European émigré described so often by East European émigrés. Think of Norman Manea's *The Hooligan's Return*, George Konrad's *Stonedial*, Milan Kundera in *Ignorance*, and many others. The awkwardness stems from the fact that there is, of course, nothing to be regretted about the passing of communism and its replacement by the somehow bland, pragmatic, materialistic life of the contemporary democratic world. But the recollection of what constituted the formative part of our youth—the period defined to a large extent by the hated regime—does evoke a sense of nostalgia. The cracks in the seemingly monolithic "totalitarian" reality in which we used to huddle and hide, the imagined journeys and sudden, childlike excitements over a poem or a scholarly essay—all this keeps reminding us that, to quote Adam Zagajewski, "we lived there / and not as strangers."

For those of us who tried to stay mentally awake and sane, literature—especially contemporary Polish literature—was a constant companion and a stimulant that helped to overcome the universal inertia. It was not an escape from reality, not life-as-a-dream, but a way to engage reality, the path to the "here-and-now," as we used to call our life at that time. Everything seemed significant, everything pointed to a shared experience, while helping at the same time to overcome its crushing weight. We felt that everything that was written, whether a long time ago or the day before, was written not only for us but also about us, the inhabitants of communist Eastern Europe in its declining (but who could know that for sure?) phase.

This does not mean we were reading everything as a veiled political treaty, an endless testimony on political oppression and rebellion. In fact, we quickly learned to reject this reductive, essentially Marxist approach to literature. We sensed quite early that the poetry of Zbigniew Herbert, Wislawa Szymborska, and, of course, Czeslaw Milosz was really about metaphysics and transcendence, not about politics and ideology. And yet it was impossible to dismiss entirely the context in which transcendence was experienced or strived for: it colored our entire perception of time, culture, self, our sense of what mattered and what made a difference.

To use a fancy metaphor, totalitarianism was something like

the opposite of Plato's sun—the Absolute that casts its light on every aspect of being. Totalitarianism was a negative sign, a dark star that held within its orbit huge chunks of human existence. Its sickening, deforming radiation, however, was not without some benefits for literature. It gave it a sense of purpose, a focus, a principle of organization. It opened a direct channel to the readers' collective mind through common fears, obsessions, myths, and hopes. It was probably no coincidence that the great phenomenon of post–World War II Polish literature known as the Polish School of Poetry–represented by, among others, the three poets mentioned above—was an exploration of a peculiar mix of history and metaphysics that seemed to define our human condition.

The representatives of the school understood writing as a search for reality, a term frequently used by Milosz. This search, however, was prompted not only by modern man's general sense of dislocation in the increasingly fragmented, incomprehensible universe, but also by a particular sense of unreality of life under communism. These poets inherited a world in ruins—in the physical, intellectual, and moral senses—and tried to find a philosophical and esthetic core that would help them rebuild it.

My generation was in a sense the generation of latecomers in this inherited domain. What did we really know? What could we compare our lives to? Our parents spent their youth in prewar Poland; they knew the horrors of the war, the postwar Stalinist terror, and the frustrated hopes of the short-lived Thaw of 1956. They had raised us in the spirit of dignified resignation and lowered expectations. What we saw around us in our adolescence was monotonous, uneventful, gray, and seemingly destined to continue forever. This state of inertia lasted until the student and intellectual protests of 1968, which were wondrous and exhilarating (I was graduating from high school and entering college in that year) but ended in the horror of repressions and spawned one of the ugliest anti-Semitic campaigns in postwar Europe. The following workers' protests of 1970 and 1976 and the formation of the Polish underground "opposition" seemed like a repetition of the familiar Polish ritual of noble futility. For a young person trying to imagine his or her future, it was a bit like looking into a dark well and seeing receding rings of grimy concrete.

At the same time there were cracks and gaps opening up in the mental wall that surrounded our lives. The exchange of ideas and information was less strictly controlled. As a result, life outside the iron curtain seemed closer, more familiar, more alluring, but also frustratingly unattainable. Books, poems, movies, music from the place known collectively as the West were trickling into our formerly isolated world, together with clothes, fads, and hairstyles. So were occasional visitors—our backpacking contemporaries in transit from San Francisco to Tangiers or from London to Lhasa. Some of us even managed to sneak out for a month or two on working vacations in London or Paris. We usually came back transformed into cultural Francophiles or Anglophiles, two distinct and often hostile tribes. The Francophiles were recognized by their pastel-colored shirts, penny loafers, and proclaimed knowledge of wines and existentialism. The Anglophiles wore thick sweaters and boots, preferred beer, and sung the praises of the

Beatles and Dirk Bogarde movies. But those infrequent furtive glimpses and fascinations only deepened our sense of being caged in a static, fading universe.

No, we weren't really that provincial. We did read Joyce, Alain Robbe-Grillet, Roland Barthes, Samuel Beckett, and Jorge Luis Borges, and we had a taste or two of American postmodern fiction. We studied structuralism, poststructuralism, and semiology and probably even took some pleasure (the pleasure of the text?) in rarefied, semiforbidden regions of Western modernism. But there was always something strange and ambivalent, perhaps even guilty, about those esthetic excursions, as if there were two kinds of literature, or two kinds of life, that we attempted to experience at the same time. There was literature as a fascinating intellectual game, a fashionable hobby, a prized possession that occupied some special niche in an educated person's life, and there was literature as the domain of vital meaning, as a heartfelt conversation or a gathering of friends.

What we read for real we read perhaps as something more than just literature. We looked for ideas, explanations, and prophecies. We canvassed the printed page for philosophy, theology, history, moral inspiration, preferably presented in the classical rhetorical mode in which form serves content, in which structure follows meaning, and in which beauty is an aspect of knowledge. Perhaps literature for us was the Great Substitute for myriads of intellectual adventures available to people in free societies? It always amazes me how few of my Polish literary friends, those living in Poland and those abroad, are still devoting most of their time and effort to literature. The vast majority of us are in politics, the media, even business.

Some have retrained themselves as lawyers, political scientists, or economists. I suspect those transformations were only partly caused by pragmatic, material considerations. In many cases they must have followed discoveries of true vocations suppressed and sublimated into the love of literature.

There is little doubt that, initially at least, what appealed to us in literary life under communism was its . . . communal character. An act of reading was an act of communication not only between the author and the reader but also between the reader and his fellow citizens — that means, his fellow readers. It was an act that restored a sense of togetherness in a deliberately fragmented, distrustful society. This condition had an impact on the way literature was received by the public and consequently on the way it was written. People expected to find allusions to issues of common concern and were ready to sing the praises of authors who met that expectation. The author, in turn, basked in the glorious role of a spiritual leader or public educator. Both sides watched one another constantly with the jealous intensity of an infatuated spouse.

In fact, this state of affairs was older than communism. It was a remnant of the nineteenth century, when Poland, erased from the map of Europe by neighboring powers, existed primarily as a cultural, literary construct. Writers were cast in the role of guardians of the national language, memory, and spirit — the domains in which the idea of "Polishness" was expected to survive until a more opportune historical moment. In the Polish mind, a writer was less an individual creator than a custodian of a common trust fund: he was expected to invest prudently, avoid unnecessary risks, and most of all preserve value.

As one might expect, those conditions favored a literary culture that was not very innovative either in form or ideology; a literature that strived to conserve and confirm what was familiar rather than scout new territories; a literature that was patiently didactic rather than rebellious. But those strictures also produced a wonderfully irreverent, contrarian streak embodied in a succession of literary eccentrics, iconoclasts, and bad boys who made a career of mocking and subverting the pious, noble national tradition.

Polish literary modernism, which coincided with regained Polish independence in 1918, was born of just such a contrarian spirit. Its best-known manifestation was the experimental prose of the "three madmen" of the interwar decades: Bruno Schulz, Stanislaw Ignacy Witkiewicz (Witkacy), and, of course, Witold Gombrowicz. I hope these essays will show how the best in contemporary Polish writing was in fact a product of a clash between the two traditions — one collectivist, didactic, and ecstatic, the other personal, skeptical, and ironic.

When I came to America in 1981, I tried to rebuild my life in a new language and new environment according to a pattern that had crystallized back in Poland. (I was thirty-one and not inclined to radical self-inventions.) With the help of a handful of good friends I settled in New York, where I planned to spend at least one year waiting for my family, which was unable to leave Warsaw because of martial law, and deciding my next move. In the meantime, I would do everything in my power to continue to associate with the same kind of people (smart, well-read, intellectually alive, but not exactly on the make) I had left behind in Warsaw. I would try to support myself through the same kinds of chores (teaching, translating, writing occasional journalistic pieces) and save some time for real, scarcely paid occupations like literary criticism.

Surprisingly, I was mostly successful. I found lovely friends, survived (barely) in a large, expensive city, and even started publishing in American newspapers and magazines. But still, not everything seemed to fit. I remember a conversation I had with an editor of one of the leading intellectual periodicals. Having glanced at my manuscript of what was supposed to be a book review, he sighed and said something like, "Jarek, you must remember that for our readers literature is important. But for God's sake, it is not the most important thing in their life!" At that moment I realized the true extent of my dislocation. I was among people who, with the exception of a handful of professionals, usually had more important things in their lives than ideas and the printed word. And that was exactly the kind of people that literature and most of literary criticism was written for!

It was a time when, owing to dramatic events in Eastern Europe, including the Solidarity uprising and martial law in Poland and growing political dissent throughout the region, the literature of Eastern Europe was very much *en vogue* in literary New York and beyond. Milosz on his frequent visits from Berkeley and Joseph Brodsky in his Greenwich Village basement apartment were the new arbiters of literary "seriousness." In Paris, Milan Kundera and Danilo Kis were grudgingly assuming a similar role. American publishers, normally scared of contemporary translations, were bringing out a whole slew of East European authors of different caliber, though with impeccable dissident credentials. And often confounded American readers wanted to know what makes East European writing work; why is it so different, obscure, abrasive? and why are they, American readers, supposed to like it or at least read it with gratitude and reverence? These were important questions because, to be sure, outside of its complex social, cultural, and historical context, East European literature often makes very little sense.

Essays contained in this book are expanded versions of review essays published in various American periodicals in response to this sudden fascination with the East European soul. I wrote them for American readers, of course, but tried to write them as if from two, sometimes quarreling points of view. On the one hand, I did not try to hide my own East European soul. I wrote as someone brought up on the myths that make Polish culture. On the other hand, I tried to look at the Polish literary landscape with the eyes of a curious but skeptical traveler. I wanted to be a guide in my native realm, but a guide who returns from his own long voyage and feels a prick of strangeness, a twinge of disbelief while approaching his hobbit hole.

I start with Schulz, Gombrowicz, and Witkiewicz, the three great reformers of Polish prose in the interwar period. Rebels and mavericks, these three set in motion a literary hurricane that is still gusting through Polish writing and starting heated cultural debates. Next, I revisit the great trinity of contemporary Polish poets — Milosz, Herbert, and Szymborska — and show that their seemingly orderly, lucid diction hides a world that is much darker, more ambiguous, and paradoxical than is usually believed. Especially Herbert, with his intricate parables and layers of irony, seemed to invite a new reading, and I was glad to learn that a similar reassessment of his work was undertaken by the Polish critic Andrzej Franaszek in his book *Ciemne zrodlo* (Dark Source), published in 1998. I also look at two most important, in my view, prose writers of the postwar period, Gustaw Herling-Grudzinski and Tadeusz Konwicki, and close with Adam Zagajewski—both the last great representative of the Polish school and a bridge to the present, postcommunist era in Polish literature.

And here the journey ends, although not because there is a dearth of interesting writing in the nearly two decades since the dark star was finally extinguished. I have been watching with great interest the ways in which the new Polish writers (some of them approaching middle age, in fact) cope with the problem long known to their Western colleagues: the deluge of words — in the media, in political discourse, in advertising—clamoring for the attention of the reading public. Theirs is probably the first generation of Polish writers who does not have ready-made answers to some of the most fundamental questions: Why do I write, and for whom? what is a writer, what is literature, really for? Some of them try to raise their voice to a level of a scream, and some try to entice the reader with intimate whispers. Most eschew abstractions and lovingly focus on details, on minute observations of the material world and individual human behavior. In poetry, they tend to draw their inspiration from the realism of the New York school, especially John Ashbery and Frank O'Hara, and from some of the more original Brits, including Seamus Heaney, David Harsent, and Hugo Williams.

Most of all, the new Polish writing loves localities — towns, neighborhoods, ethnic regions — which hide accumulated memories and unexpected troves of human stories. This new search for "little homelands" brought us the Danzig/Gdansk of Pawel Huelle and Stefan Chwin, the Carpathian boondocks of Andrzej Stasiuk, the living, thinking stones of Magdalena Tulli's Warsaw, the decrepit suburban "projects" of Dorota Maslowska, and the Polish-Ukrainian borderland of the poetry of Eugeniusz Tkaczyszyn-Dycki.

Much of this new literature is written in reaction to what younger writers consider the exaggerated metaphysical ambitions of their predecessors. They prefer to concentrate on the more modest task of exploring lesser-known aspects of human experience through the unique medium of the language. I must confess that I much admire their cocky disdain for their elders' *Angst* and *Drang*, in which I detect a new form of freedom and a new brand of courage.

But I also believe that the period touched upon in this book — the time, roughly, from the end of World War I through the end of communism — stands out as a product of a unique confluence of historical forces, literary sensibilities, and individual genius. Its importance relates directly to what Susan Sontag once called "the perpetuation of the project of literature itself." This book, of course, cannot give full credit to its complexity and scope. I hope, however, that it may encourage some readers to further study what for me remains one of the most fascinating literary adventures of the second half of the twentieth century.

ACKNOWLEDGMENTS

Most chapters of the book had their origin as review essays and expand upon, or incorporate in various measures, previously published materials. An earlier version of "The Prisoner of Myth" appeared in *The New Republic* (October 7, 1996). "The Transforming Self" combines and expands two review essays from *The New Republic*, "The Transforming Self" (June 20, 1988) and "Unsentimental Journey" (December 12, 1994). An earlier version of "Modernism to Madness" appeared in *The New Republic* (July 10, 1996). "Testament of an Exile" is a version of "Beauty and Certainty" (*The New Republic*, April 12, 1999) expanded with some new material as well as fragments of an earlier essay, "Voice of Exile" (*New York Review of Books*, February 27, 1986). "The Darkness of Mr. Cogito" is mostly new but incorporates elements of a short review, "Time Must Have a Stop" (*Los Angeles Times Book Review*, August 8, 1999). "The Power of Preserving" weaves together material from two review essays, "The Revenge of the Mortal Hand" (*New York Review of Books*, October 21, 1982) and "Hunger of Memory" (*Los Angeles Times Book Review*, May 17, 1998). "Sleepless in Naples" includes material from a review of Gustaw Herling's *The Island: Three Tales* in the *Boston Sunday Globe* (January 3, 1993) and from a review of *The Noonday Cemetery* by the same author in *Los Angeles Times Book Review* (September 1, 2003).

"Polish Endgame" combines two review essays, "The Polish Wake" (*New York Review of Books*, March 4, 1982) and "Not With a Bang" (*The New Republic*, November 21, 1983). "To Hear the Sound of Everything" owes some passages (and the whole book its title) to a short review, "Between Fire and Sleep" (*Los Angeles Times Book Review*, February 1, 1998).

I owe much more than ordinary gratitude to three extraordinary editors, with whom I had a chance to work when those essays appeared in their original form. They are, in the chronological order in which I met them, Robert Silvers of the *New York Review of Books*, Steve Wasserman of *Los Angeles Times Book Review*, and Leon Wieseltier of *The New Republic*. A dear departed friend, Susan Sontag, dared me to write in a language that was not my own. Jonathan Brent, of Yale University Press, deserves special praise for his heroic faith and patience. Of course, nothing at all would be possible without the encouragement and love of my family.

One of the most frequently recounted biographies in the history of Polish literature is known primarily for its ending. On November 19, 1942, a Gestapo officer shot and killed a fifty-year-old man in the Drohobycz ghetto. The victim, one of more than two hundred Jews who were murdered on that Black Thursday, was Bruno Schulz, a local high school teacher and artist and the author of two slim volumes of dreamlike prose that a few years earlier had been hailed as one of the most original achievements of Polish literature in the twentieth century. It is hard to guess what this timid, cautious person was doing in the streets during a German killing spree, one of numerous such "wild actions" that preceded the final solution. According to one version of the event, Schulz had decided to attempt to escape from Drohobycz and was going to the local *Judenrat* to purchase his ration of bread. Others say that, ill and dejected, he was roaming the streets as if looking for death. He appears to have fallen victim to a feud between two local Nazi satraps. His body remained in the street until sunset, when he was secretly buried by some friends; his grave has never been found.

A few months earlier, in Nazi-occupied Warsaw, an eighteen-year-old Polish poet named Jerzy Ficowski read one of Schulz's books, published shortly before the outbreak of the war. Ficowski, who died in 2006, said he experienced a sense of immediate, almost mystical connection with the writer and a conviction that Schulz must be "the kind of genius who sometimes creates great religious systems, or a magician and master of black arts, whose predecessors were burned at medieval stakes."[1] Ficowski did not know that Schulz, resettled into the ghetto in Galicia and furnished with a certificate that protected him as a "necessary Jew," had been surviving for some time as an artist-slave in the service of a brutal SS man named Felix Landau. Landau took a fancy to his drawings, made him paint his portraits and decorate his villa, and secured artistic assignments for him for the German institutions in the town. (Some of Schulz's frescos survived the war. In 2001 they were snatched from Drohobycz by Yad Vashem and surreptitiously transported to Israel, causing an international furor.)

Having learned of Schulz's death, Ficowski decided to preserve as much as possible of his hero's legacy. He wished to salvage and to reconstruct Schulz from scraps of surviving documents and letters and from the memories of those who knew him. He became the self-appointed custodian of the writer's work and life. Ficowski, who lived in Warsaw in an apartment filled with Schulz memorabilia, is also known as a poet, a translator from Yiddish, a specialist in Gypsy literature, and an author of books for children. His cycle of poems "Odczytanie popiolow" (*A Reading of Ashes*) is one of the most powerful literary testimonies to the Holocaust written in Polish by a non-Jew.[2] And yet, despite his own considerable literary achievement, Ficowski is defined chiefly by his Schulzian obsession. He declared himself "a reader of a single book, one for which no rival has emerged," a "personal and disquieting bible" that speaks about "the secret essence of things which transcend their own limitations" — in other words, the Book of Schulz.

Thus, whatever we know about Schulz, we know from Ficowski, whose biographical-critical essay *Regiony Wielkiej Herezji* (Regions of the Great Heresy), the result of a lifelong and almost religious devotion to the strange writer from Drohobycz, was published in Poland in 1967, only a few years after Schulz's own prose was resurrected by Polish publishers following decades of neglect.[3] It was soon followed by *Ksiega Listow* (The Book of Letters,) a collection of Schulz's correspondence edited by Ficowski, and two other books devoted to more recently discovered letters, writings, and testimonies.[4] The English edition of *Regions of the Great Heresy: Bruno Schulz, A Biographical Portrait* is an expanded version of its Polish predecessor and includes material from Ficowski's other publications on Schulz.

It is hard to overestimate the service Ficowski has performed with his uncommon dedication. He has managed to preserve — not only for Polish literature, but also for world literature — a very great writer and also substantial fragments of his world, the Galician-Jewish-Polish-Ukrainian mélange that was completely wiped out by World War II and its brutal aftermath. It is quite possible that without Ficowski there would be no Schulz, just as without Max Brod there would be no Franz Kafka. And yet the Schulz that we have is distinctly Ficowski's Schulz — his own reconstruction of a writer and an individual who, from the strictly factual standpoint, remains a puzzle, a subject of conjecture, hypothesis, and invention. Ficowski is not only the archaeologist of Schulz's life; he is also the creator of the Schulzian myth.

In this respect, too, the analogy with Brod's impact upon the reception of Kafka comes to mind. For the myth of Schulz and the myth of Kafka display striking similarities. They are both varieties of the modernist myth of the artist as a dark hero, a neurotic, a misfit rejected and maligned by the philistine society in which he miserably lives, humbled by circumstances but spiritually unvanquished, bearing cryptic revelations beyond the comprehension of conventional reason. In *Regions of the Great Heresy*, Ficowski declares that he is not interested in a reasoned analysis of Schulz's prose and quotes his idol, who wrote in a letter to his friend and fellow writer Stanislaw Ignacy Witkiewicz in 1935, "I think that the rationalization of the vision of things rooted in the work of art is like the demasking of actors. . . . In the work of art the umbilical cord is not yet cut that joins it to the whole of the problem. The blood of the mystery is still circulating; the ends of the vessels escape into the surrounding night and return full of a dark fluid."[5]

Ficowski seemed to subscribe to this romantic view without reservation. "The essence of the work," he remarks in *Regions of the Great Heresy*, "remains unattainable, always happily eluding the critics' scalpels and microscopes." And since any "close reading" of the text is tantamount to sacrilege, what remains is the close reading of the artist's life, the study of the "correlations between the man and the writer, the life and the work, the actual events and the artistic creation." Ficowski's Schulz is an emblematic modern artistic sufferer, not unlike Brod's Kafka: a sickly, misunderstood, lonely, inhibited man who faces reality with the naïveté and the helplessness — and the privileged intuitions — of a child seeking refuge in the magic gardens of his imagination. "A profound inferiority complex accompanied him all his life," Ficowski writes, "for which his artistic creativity later became a partial remedy, but never a complete liberation. . . . The shyness or embarrassment which rarely left him precluded closeness with others and intensified the growing sense of isolation that tormented him from childhood: his increasingly hermetic solitude."

Schulz, according to Ficowski, was "consumed by fears and complexes" and surrounded by hostile, insensitive people from whom he was forced to conceal "the literary and artistic fruit of his spiritual entanglements and complications." One of these "complications" was apparently his masochistic sexuality, which found expression in his erotic drawings. About this subject Ficowski is more reticent than about others, but he suggests that his hero suffered from pathological submissiveness and passivity that prevented him from escaping his provincial environment, his dreary job, and eventually his death in Nazi-occupied Drohobycz. This is now the Schulz of legend. But the truth is more complicated, as always. Indeed, even the facts gathered by Ficowski allow us to sketch a different, though no less intriguing, portrait of the writer and the artist.

Bruno Schulz was born in 1892 into an assimilated Jewish family. His father, Jacob, was a merchant, while his mother, Henrietta, came from an affluent industrialist family. Schulz's native town, Drohobycz, at that time in the Austro-Hungarian empire, was not at all a somnolent shtetl, as it is often described, but a vibrant provincial town with a theater and a red light district, later portrayed so memorably by Schulz in his story "The Street of Crocodiles." Drohobycz owed its relative prosperity to oilfields discovered in nearby Boryslaw in the foothills of the Carpathian Mountains, and its outer suburbs were dotted with the luxurious villas of the local plutocracy. The proximity of Truskawiec, a fashionable spa frequented by vacationers from Krakow, Lvov, and Warsaw, contributed to Drohobycz's peculiar mixture of the provincial and the cosmopolitan.

Drohobycz was sometimes called a town and a half because it was supposedly half-Polish, half-Jewish, and half-Ukrainian. In fact, Jews constituted almost half of the population, the other half being divided more or less evenly between Poles and Ukrainians. After the war, Drohobycz became a stock of legends among its Polish and Jewish diaspora, an epitome of Galician charm and multiethnic geniality. (According to one account, the funeral of a beloved Drohobycz rabbi was attended by crowds of Polish and Ukrainian mourners.) But the Polish-Jewish writer Henryk Grynberg, in his book *Drohobycz, Drohobycz*, paints a much darker picture of the relations between the communities that shared this place on the eve of the catastrophe.[6] According to testimonies gathered by Grynberg, Polish and Ukrainian nationalisms simmered throughout the interwar years and sometimes erupted into open hostility, with Poles and Ukrainians pitted against each other and against the always-punishable Jews. Still, Drohobycz under Polish rule did not experience pogroms or any major incidents of nationalist violence. It certainly helped when Jews, such as the Schulz family, did not manifest their religious difference. Bruno, who later formally left the Jewish religious community, was named after the Christian patron of his birthday. He never openly converted to Christianity, but witnesses say that while accompanying his mostly Catholic students to church (as part of his teacher's duties), he would genuflect in front of the crucifix. All this, of course, seems like an idyll in comparison with what was soon to follow.

The young Schulz excelled in school and quickly demonstrated his artistic talents. His teachers encouraged him to pursue his interest in the visual arts, which seemed to be his main vocation, and his school proudly sponsored the printing of a postcard featuring one of his works.[7] Later the explicitly sexual content of many of his drawings scandalized the conservative elements of the Drohobycz community, but there is no evidence that Schulz treated his art as especially personal or shameful or that he tried to hide it from the world. He frequently exhibited his drawings in Warsaw, Lvov, Krakow, and Truskawiec, presented them as gifts to friends and relatives, and sold them in self-published folios. He treated them, in other words, with a measure of professional detachment. He often drew his own face on the dwarfish, half-human creatures crawling at the feet of his beautiful, pouting women, but he also liked to depict his friends and acquaintances in similar states of abjection. (He created a minor scandal when someone recognized his wife among the naked prostitutes in one of the more lascivious drawings.) But those familiar with the expressionist style of the time, which clearly influenced Schulz, must have understood those excesses as a calculated erotic impishness. In those days, perversion was an artistic fashion. Vienna was not too far away, and even Drohobycz had to maintain its standards of decadence.

Like his father, Schulz suffered from poor health, which interfered with his studies and his creativity. He was afflicted by phobias and anxieties — and yet his life was hardly as sorrowful as is often assumed. In fact, most of his days passed in relative comfort. The Schulz family was sufficiently well-off to allow the artistically inclined son to pursue his interests without worrying about gainful employment. After graduating from high school Schulz studied architecture in Lvov. A bout of illness and the outbreak of World War I forced him to return to Drohobycz. A year later his father died, at the age of sixty-nine. Soon afterward, excused from military service on account of his health, Schulz traveled to Vienna, where he attempted to resume his architectural studies, although his stay in the capital of the crumbling Austro-Hungarian empire lasted only six months. Back in Drohobycz, he joined a group of local young intellectuals, artists, and musicians called Kalleia, or "beautiful things"; practiced his graphic craft; and read voraciously from the library and the bookstore of the father of one of his closest friends.

Though he is often described as a loner, Schulz was in fact a gregarious fellow. He was always surrounded by brilliant, devoted, and often influential friends, especially sophisticated women of artistic ambitions. Some of them remained his lifelong correspondents and promoters, and one of them, a Polish-Jewish poet named Debora Vogel, encouraged him to think seriously about writing. Later, when Schulz became known in avant-garde circles in Warsaw, his close friends included not only Witkiewicz, but also the caustic Witold Gombrowicz and the grande dame of Polish letters, Zofia Nalkowska, whose salon (and bedroom) he visited during his stays in Warsaw. It was Nalkowska's enthusiasm that opened doors at the best literary periodicals and the avant-garde publishing house Roj (The Hive), which brought out both of Schulz's books as well as Gombrowicz's groundbreaking novel *Ferdydurke*, with a design by Schulz on its cover.

Schulz's correspondence indicates that he was by no means an innocent about the workings of literary life, and though he was lacking in natural resourcefulness he could nonetheless manage his career with a degree of professionalism and cunning. We see him systematically trying to break into literary Warsaw and to meet the right people. In one letter he openly solicits a favorable review for an acquaintance who, he admits, may be useful to him. He could be quite effective in pestering his friends for help in getting grants and writing assignments, and he met with a surprising amount of kindness. Even the usually pitiless Gombrowicz, who occasionally taunted Schulz for what he considered artistic affectations, displayed an uncharacteristic protectiveness toward his much older colleague. Schulz's famous letters — mostly lyrical and literary, sometimes including credo-like explanations of his ideas about art — can be surprisingly businesslike. They also betray a self-centered personality preoccupied almost exclusively with his own spiritual ventures, his writing, and the practical problems of his life. He rarely takes an interest in other people's dilemmas. He speaks about his desire for solitude and silence, but he longs for an ideal camaraderie of kindred souls, "partners in discovery," "one or two people who would not constrain me," "sensitive souls one does not have to close oneself from, or translate oneself into a foreign language." Like most writers, in sum, he seeks not friends but admirers. He was forever in need of reassurance.

There is also an unmistakable note of self-pity running through Schulz's letters, especially after he was finally forced to get a job as an arts and crafts teacher in order to support himself and his widowed sister. He saw it as an undeserved punishment and an unbearable burden. "So much mechanical, soulless work for someone who could do other things — that is after all a great injustice," he wrote to a fellow schoolteacher. "My nervous system has a fastidiousness and delicacy which has not matured to the demands of a life denied the sanction of art," he remarked melodramatically on another occasion. "I am afraid this school year will kill me." The torment of teaching was also a handy explanation for his prolonged periods of despondency and his increasing problems with summoning his creative powers. Ficowski declares his full sympathy with his hero's suffering: "A mythologue-artist in the role of an overworked secondary school teacher was the contradiction and violation inflicted upon Schulz's own identity."

And yet this "violation" was also a guarantee of the security Schulz needed as much as he needed the "sanction of art." It is hard to imagine a person more unsuited to a bohemian way of life and more averse to risk. "In order to create," he confided in a friend, "I must have a particularly kindly and encouraging climate around me — good faith in myself, quiet, safety":

lacking independent means, in other words, he needed a cozy
sinecure. He obtained the job on the strength of his artistic
achievement rather than his education or his experience, and he
really expected an "idyll among professions" that would be
appropriate for "people possessed of some mission, some lofty
but unprofitable task." It turned out to be just a job, but the
money was adequate, and tenure—which Schulz received after
a few years of employment—guaranteed an economic sanctuary in a time of general uncertainty and widespread poverty.

It seems almost certain that his job, so maligned in many of
his letters, was for Schulz a perverse source of satisfaction. His
students remember him as an inspiring, if distracted, teacher,
one who knew how to encourage the more gifted among them
while dazzling others with improvised fairy tales. Ficowski observes that "for an eccentric, Schulz enjoyed a considerable
degree of respect," and his principals seemed to take great pride
in his literary and artistic achievements. His publications, his
exhibitions, and his awards were cited in the school memory
books. Schulz was recognized and even celebrated by the more
sophisticated among his colleagues and his neighbors.

The legend of his slavish attachment to Drohobycz—a kind
of self-imprisonment in the Galician backwater—also has little
support from the facts. No doubt Schulz needed Drohobycz as
the backdrop for his fantasies. His imagination required the
excitement of the familiar so as to perform its feats of defamil-
iarization and to transform it into the phantasmagoric landscapes of his stories. He often spoke about his hometown with
affection, but he could also be cruel and disdainful about it,
calling it a "death from monotony, growing boredom, terrible

vomiting from the sterility of life." Anyway, he spent considerable amounts of time outside Drohobycz. He vacationed in
nearby Truskawiec, which is the setting of some of his stories,
but also in the more trendy and artistic Zakopane. He traveled
to Lvov and Krakow, and after his literary debut he was a frequent visitor to Warsaw. Since his youthful sojourn in Vienna
he was never tempted to return there, and for obvious reasons
he carefully avoided Berlin; but he spent several weeks in Paris,
on a failed attempt to launch his international career. He made
the mistake of trying to take Paris in August, when the city
is empty, but he brought back memories of grand museums
and Parisian women, "those of proper society and cocottes,
their free manner, the tempo of life." He even took a three-day
cruise on the Baltic Sea and spent a day in Stockholm. For a
provincial East European of modest means and with a proclivity to peace and predictability, Schulz had a rather interesting life and was in this respect more fortunate than many of the
modernist writers and artists of his time — until the outbreak of
the war, of course, when the true horror began for Schulz and
millions of others.

Even though the myth of the "subterranean" Schulz, under-
appreciated and unloved, should be treated with caution, there
is no doubt that the author of *Sanatorium Under the Sign of
the Hourglass* was a profoundly unhappy man.[8] What is more,
the period of his most acute despondency seem to have coincided with the beginning of his literary career and the praise
with which his work was greeted by most prominent literary
voices of his day. Ficowski suggests that Schulz's depression was

caused by his inability to deal with his new public status and by his frustration at not having enough time to proceed with his literary projects. It is possible, however, that the writer — in his midforties and still on the threshold of a literary career — was displaying the first symptoms of artistic exhaustion. Perhaps one should look for the source of Schulz's anguish not in the circumstances of his life, but in the particular nature of his artistic sensibility. He may have become a victim of his own imagination, which trapped him in an invented world that was beginning to lose its magic.

Among his contemporaries Schulz is most often compared with Kafka. In truth, the two writers are almost polar opposites; and Ficowski shrewdly insists upon the dissimilarity in *Regions of the Great Heresy*: "Schulz was a builder of a reality-asylum that was a marvelous 'intensification of the taste of the world'; Kafka was an inhabitant and propagator of a world of terror, an ascetic hermit awaiting a miracle of justice that never came. Schulz was a metaphysician garbed in all the wealth of color; Kafka was a mystic in a hair shirt of worldly denials. Schulz was a creator and ruler of compensatory Myth; Kafka was the Sisyphean seeker of the Absolute."

One may object that there is a fair amount of terror in Schulz's world as well, but it is certainly true that Kafka strips the world naked, whereas Schulz drapes it in layers of fantasy. Kafka's heroes, though helpless and confused, are not in doubt about the difference between the self and the world, and their struggle for justice is a struggle to maintain this difference. Schulz's narrator, by contrast, strives to obliterate that barrier and to create a reality that would be a seamless blending of the ego and the world. The difference of purpose between the two writers is obvious even in their language: there is Kafka's reticence and concreteness, his striving for semantic precision, which is one of the self's defenses against abstraction; and there is Schulz's effusiveness, mistiness, impressionistic excess, which render an object or an event indistinguishable from the mental state it evokes.

The unfortunate pairing of the two writers is partially due to the fact that the first Polish translation of *The Trial* bears Schulz's name, although most probably it was done by his fiancée, Jozefina Szelinska. In the foreword to the translation, Schulz asserts that in Kafka's prose "for the first time the magic of poetry has created a species of parallel reality, a fictional body upon which mystical experience can be demonstrated." But Schulz is talking about himself, not about Kafka. When Gregor Samsa metamorphoses into a terrible insect, his transformation does not carry us into a parallel reality in which such occurrences are commonplace; instead it throws into relief the familiar world of daily concerns, hopes, and disappointments in which real Samsas, as well as most of us, actually live. Kafka is sensitive to everything that is irrational and illusory in life, but he confronts this irrationality in a cool, highly analytical mode, so as to demonstrate, not unlike Gombrowicz, how absurdity imperceptibly invades and subverts the most ordinary situations. For Schulz, on the other hand, the irrational and the fantastic are means of escape from the self and from the struggles in which it is constantly embroiled. That is why Schulz cannot understand why Jozef K. is "clinging to his human reason instead of surrendering unconditionally" and following the two strangers to whatever fate they may have prepared for him. Schulz's closest literary kin is probably Rainer Maria Rilke, whom he read avidly. In Rilke's poetry and prose he recognized his own longing for "a very quiet, self-isolated world . . . narcissism, solitude, seclusion inside a glass globe," and he believed that poetry draws its energy from the subconscious, "the tangled, deaf mass unformulated in us," which can "rise to the surface wonderfully distilled." The metaphors of the two writers often display surprising similarities. When Malte Laurids Brigge, Rilke's flaneur, walks down an empty street, he notices that "its emptiness had gotten bored and pulled my steps out from under my feet and clattered around in them, all over the street, as if they were wooden clogs."[9] A similar transformation of emptiness occurs when the young protagonist of Schulz's story "August" observes a sleeping woman: "And, as if taking advantage of her sleep, the silence talked, the yellow, bright, evil silence delivered its monologue, argued, and loudly spoke its vulgar, maniacal soliloquy. Maria's time — the time imprisoned in her soul — had left her and — terribly real — filled the room, vociferous and hellish in the bright silence of the morning, rising from the noisy mill of the clock like a cloud of bad flour, powdery flour, the stupid flour of madmen."

The typical Schulzian metaphor — often no more than a simile or analogy — endows objects, shapes, natural phenomena, and even abstract notions such as time and space with their own secret vitality. The writer leads us into a world in which burrs are "enormous witches, shedding their voluminous skirts in broad daylight," and apricots shelter "the core of long after-noons," and chandeliers blacken and wilt "like old thistles," and interiors "reflect their dark turbulent past," and mirrors cast "secret glances," friezes "panic," and wallpapers whisper and dream, while unmade, crumpled beds stand "like deep boats waiting to sail into the dank and confusing labyrinths of some dark starless Venice."

This is the deeply personal, lyrical, and animistic universe of Joseph, the awestruck child-narrator of Schulz's stories, who is obviously named after the biblical diviner of dreams. Two other main characters, always portrayed through Joseph's eyes, are the father, a magician conducting strange experiments "in the unexplored regions of existence," and a maid, "slim-legged Adela," who brings erotic tension into Joseph's world and whose ostentatious sexuality repeatedly spoils the father's magic. Occasionally we encounter also Joseph's mother, an affectionate but uncomprehending woman, uneasy and embarrassed by the zone of secrecy surrounding her husband. The father, Jacob (this was the name of Schulz's real father), is certainly the most puzzling protagonist of the Schulzian universe. He fascinates his son as someone who is in touch with the "roots of existence," a person capable of conjuring "unknown forms of life." But he is also distant, secretive, a bit menacing, "completely submerged in an inaccessible sphere." Sometimes it is suggested that he is "already lost, sold and surrendered to the other sphere," perhaps dead and revisiting his son's dreamscapes under fantastic guises — as a stuffed condor, a giant cockroach, a cooked crab. In the story "Sanatorium Under the Sign of the Hourglass," he is simultaneously a bedridden, dying old man and a robust businessman enthusiastically pursuing his suspicious ventures. His chief quality seems to consist in inhabiting several worlds simultaneously, being present and absent, glorious and miserable, existing in a condition of constant transition that brings a thrill of excitement into his son's world but also a terrible foreboding.

Moving within the orbit of the father's dark star, young Joseph conducts his own explorations of reality's hidden side. In a garden overgrown with weeds he encounters a sylvan deity who turns out to be a defecating drifter. He spies on a retarded girl who in her trance appears to him "like a pagan idol." He pursues an aloof, beautiful girl named Bianca who lives in one of the opulent villas on the outskirts of the town, and he rides through a winter landscape in a cart drawn by a horse that dies at the end of their trip and turns into a toy. During these peregrinations, familiar places — streets surrounding the city square, school corridors, even his home — turn into endless labyrinths, while time splits into parallel strands, slows down, or becomes dense and incongruous like time in a dream.

All these transformations create a kind of glowing impressionistic tapestry that sometimes strikes the reader as uncommonly beautiful, disquieting, and original. But how did this world come to be? What is its motivation and its purpose? Most critics point to what appears to be Schulz's commentary on his art scattered throughout his writings and expressed most fully in his essay "The Mythologizing of Reality," which was published in 1936. "The essence of Reality," writes Schulz, "is Meaning or Sense. What lacks Sense is, for us, not reality. Every fragment of reality lives by virtue of partaking in a universal Sense." There was a time, he continues, when every word contained that universal Sense, leading us directly to a "great universal whole." Later, words lost this holistic quality but are striving to regain it by reaching out in many directions, "like the cut-up snake in the legend." This striving of the word toward wholeness is, for Schulz, the very definition of poetry: "Poetry happens when short-circuits of sense occur between words, a sudden regeneration of the primeval myth." Human search for knowledge and meaning, in fact every mental operation, is, according to Schulz, a burrowing among half-forgotten ancient narratives, "stories" that still linger in our subconsciousness. The poet's task is to reach into this deposit and to restore "conductivity" to words. "Language is man's metaphysical organ," says Schulz, because reality is the reflection of the word, not the other way around.

Notions such as "Sense," "Meaning," and "Myth," as well as a powerfully postlapsarian feeling about his own time, appear regularly in Schulz's writing, although it is extremely difficult to define them precisely. (In places Schulz sounds uncannily like his contemporary Walter Benjamin.) Sometimes it looks as if the writer is speaking of nothing less than the search for a Gnostic "ur-Text," God's original Logos that created the world and, according to some beliefs, still resonates within the world. In a letter to the Polish poet Julian Tuwim, Schulz writes, "You have taught me that each state of the soul pursued sufficiently far into its depth leads through the straits and canals of the world—into mythology." In the same letter he also speaks about childhood as "The Age of Genius" (later the title of one of his stories), the time of prerational unity of the self and the world, when "all things breathed the radiance of divine colors," and one was able to feel the closeness of the Sense in a mystical, nonverbal way.

In the story "Spring," in which the lovelorn Joseph reinvents history for the benefit of his beloved Bianca, Schulz addresses his reader, charging him directly to search for "the limitless possibilities of being" by descending into the uncharted regions of the subconscious, into the "labyrinths of depth" where "a great many old tales and ancient sagas have been collected, when too many whispers have been gathered underground, inarticulate pulp and dark nameless things that existed before words." In the story "The Book," Joseph is convinced that some time ago, in his early childhood, the mysterious all-germinating scripture was in fact in his possession: "The Book lay still and the wind opened it softly like a huge cabbage rose; the petals, one by one, eyelid under eyelid, all blind, velvety, and dreamy, slowly disclosed a blue pupil, a colored peacock's heart, or a chattering nest of hummingbirds." In comparison with "the Book," even the Bible appears to him a mere "clumsy falsification." In the end, Schulz's protagonist discovers that the mystical volume was only a pile of old illustrated magazines, full of strange stories and intriguing, earthly pictures.

Like most of those who write about Schulz, Ficowski tends to accept the writer's mystical self-interpretation. "His creation," he writes in *Regions of the Great Heresy*, "was hovering over an impenetrable secret." But I doubt that Schulz really was an aspiring adept in search of the Mysteries. It is true that he seems to postulate a unity of matter and spirit, a life force permeating even inanimate objects; but his visions develop as a series of unconnected impressionistic images that never cohere into a larger pattern suggestive of a deeper metaphysical order. His baroque metaphors, his brilliant and innovative linguistic clusters certainly "renew" the world, but they do not discover anything about its nature, origin, or destiny. It is more likely that the search for a "primeval myth" is for Schulz merely an alibi for a free play of imagination. His real goal is not the philosophical or religious probing of life's depths, but the experience of life in an intensely sensual and radiantly aesthetic way.

Indeed, Schulz himself seems to treat his own alibi with a measure of distrust. The magical kingdom of his prose, with its decorative richness, seems always on the verge of collapse or self-parody. Like the "cinnamon shops" in one of his stories, the world impressed in the mind of the protagonist resembles an old curiosity shop in which cheap trinkets glitter for a time like treasure before they return to their shoddy quotidian form. This strange coexistence of trashiness and magic was often interpreted as a clash between two antagonistic forces: the power of the imagination that lifts the hero into the realm of the spirit, and the downward pull of the degraded, materialistic reality of the new industrial age that intruded upon the quiet town of Drohobycz, represented, respectively, by the father, the guardian of the vanishing world of old, and the licentious, provocative Adela, who constantly distracts him with her legs.

Ficowski accepts this dichotomy and suggests that Schulz tried to escape the encroaching materialism and the vulgar physicality by constructing an imaginary, hypothetical Arcadia of childhood. In fact, the opposition in Schulz's prose appears much less obvious: the shabby and the sublime (to borrow

Adam Zagajewski's terms) are almost indistinguishable. When, in "The Street of Crocodiles," Schulz describes the district of illicit pleasures and suspicious transactions, the "parasitical quarter" vibrates with the same magic and endless transformative possibilities as the more innocent visions of young Joseph. The fundamental deceptiveness of this world, the "sham comedy," the "tawdry charm" of its colorful putrefaction seem the very conditions that make a Schulzian conjuring possible. They also communicate the reverse side of his creations: their palpable sadness, the sense of frustration and futility that colors the writer's private world. When Schulz describes the Street of Crocodiles, he may be writing about the workings of his own imagination:

> Let us say it bluntly: the misfortune of that area is that nothing ever succeeds there, nothing can ever reach a definite conclusion. . . . It is in fact no more than a fermentation of desires, prematurely aroused and therefore impotent and empty. It is an atmosphere of excessive facility, every whim flies high, a passing excitement swells into an empty parasitic growth; a light gray vegetation of fluffy weeds, of colorless poppies sprouts forth, made from a weightless fabric of nightmares and hashish. . . . Nowhere as much as there do we feel threatened by possibilities, shaken by the nearness of fulfillment, pale and faint with the delightful rigidity of realization. And that is as far as it goes.
>
> Having exceeded a certain point of tension, the tide stops and begins to ebb, the atmosphere becomes unclear and troubled, possibilities fade and decline into a void, the crazy gray poppies of excitement scatter into ashes.

"And that is as far as it goes": it is a fitting motto, almost an epitaph, for the Schulzian fantasy. At a closer look his seemingly boundless world appears confined to the point of claustrophobia. Every movement leads to a dead end or brings us back to the point of departure. The narrator of the story "Sanatorium Under the Sign of the Hourglass" visits what appears to be the place of his father's afterlife only to discover a world in which everything has already happened and the present seems to be no more than anticipated memory. The future does not exist in this world, and therefore there is no expectation, no chance of enrichment, no discovery, no possibility of escape, only "passing excitement" and "parasitic growth."

This curious split within Schulz's vision is probably the most important characteristic of his writing. He wishes to believe in the omnipotence of heroic, sovereign imagination and treats creativity as a form of religious revelation; but he suspects that what we think, dream, and remember—our entire "internal" life—may be made of trash and that our supposed freedom of imagination is just a solipsistic prison.

The proximity, or even the sameness, of the shabby and the sublime is the subject of Schulz's story-essay "Treatise on Tailor's Dummies or the Second Book of Genesis." In a lecture delivered to Adela and two seamstress girls, the father states that "creation is the privilege of all spirits," and man should claim the role of the Demiurge's partner, or even competitor. He should attempt to breath his own spirit into the world because "there is no dead matter" and "lifelessness is only a disguise behind which hide unknown forms of life." The search for the Sense, the resurrection of the forgotten "Myth," is nothing less than the second Genesis, in which man assumes the role of a cocreator, or rather a cofabulator, of the universe.

At a certain point the father's call for a new demiurgy of man assumes a chillingly nihilistic tone: "Homicide is not a sin. It is sometimes a necessary violence on resistant and ossified forms of existence which have ceased to be amusing. In the interests of an important and fascinating experiment, it can even become meritorious. Here is the starting point of a new apologia for sadism."

After this surprising declaration, the father admits that the original "recipes" used by the real Demiurge may be beyond man's reach. "But this is unnecessary," he continues, "because even if the classical methods of creation should prove inaccessible for evermore, there still remain illegal methods, an infinity of heretical and criminal methods." In his competition with God, man should "give priority to trash," should yield to his natural passion for shabby, imperfect materials, "for colored tissue, for papier-mâché, for distemper, for oakum and sawdust." Man's creativity, according to the father, belongs to the "lower sphere," which he calls *generatio aequivoca*. His efforts would produce short-lived, illusory forms, "colorful and exuberant mildew," "a fantastic growth, like a beautiful rash." In another story, "Second Fall," the father compares beauty to a disease, "the result of a mysterious infection, a dark forerunner of decomposition, which rises from the depth of perfection and is saluted by perfection with signs of the deepest bliss."

Schulz's universe seems to be constructed according to the father's directive. Every intense experience suggests simultaneously a mystical revelation and a sham. In the story "Cinnamon Shops," Joseph accompanies his parents to a theater, where he observes a huge, painted stage curtain that appears to him "like the sky of another firmament." When a gust of air moves the curtain, it sends a tremor across the canvas that breaks his illusion, but at the same time it causes "the vibration of reality which, in metaphysical moments, we experience as the glimmer of revelation." Has the view of the crudely painted curtain led the boy to a mystical experience? or has it produced merely a "passing excitement"? Is the illustrated magazine in "The Book" a portal to the secret universe? or does it evoke in the young narrator empty "fermentation of desires"? It is probably Schulz's indecision in these matters that is the source of his verbal inventiveness, his unstoppable rush of metaphors that are always trying to insinuate more than words can express.

Yet the same ambiguity is also responsible for something sad and unfulfilled that lurks behind this fever of creativity. Schulz's imaginary kingdom enchants, but it also stifles. The reader is attracted to this domain and wants to explore it with somehow voyeuristic curiosity but also feels it wise to plot a route of retreat. Perhaps this was the true source of the growing sense of disappointment and isolation visible in Schulz's letters after the publication of his works. We know he found it increasingly difficult to find satisfaction in the creations of his mind, to achieve a "revaluation of life through poetry."

Ficowski's claims to the contrary notwithstanding, Schulz likely abandoned his novel *Messiah*, which is probably the most frequently discussed nonexistent book in the history of literature. But more generally, I think, he was unable to break out of the prison of his imagination. He remarked in a letter to one of his friends, "It seems to me that the world, life, is important for me solely as material for artistic creation. The moment I cannot utilize life creatively—it becomes either terrible and dangerous, or morally vapid for me." To say that life unredeemed by art becomes "morally vapid" is to confess that one is living in a hell of aestheticism.

Schulz was clearly aware that this categorical imperative to transform everything into art is a human deficiency. He considered himself incapable of love, and there is very little compassion in his writing. Only occasionally, in the stories about the retarded middle-aged man named Dodo and the crippled teenage boy Eddie, are we shown other human beings in a way that suggests their own personal dramas. Schulz hoped that by marrying Jozefina Szelinska he might be cured of his pathological detachment. In one of his letters he confided to a friend that "my fiancée constitutes my participation in life; through her I am a person, not just a lemur and kobold," and he confesses to being lost in "inhuman realms, barren underworlds of fantasy." When his engagement broke off, he only half-jokingly considered the life of debauchery as the next best thing to his isolation. His late letters testify to a struggle with the crushing limits of his mind and also to the possibility of liberation from it: "The peculiarity and exceptionality of my inner process closed me off hermetically, rendered [me] insensitive, averse to invasion of the world. Now I open myself as if for the second time to the world and all would be well were it not for that fear and inner hesitation, as before a risky venture, leading God knows where." In a letter written in 1937 he reported that "what shut me off from the world's onslaughts recedes gently into the background and I, like an insect released from its cocoon, exposed to the tempest of an alien light and the winds of heaven, commit myself to the elements, in a way for the first time."

We shall probably never know what occasioned this need to break out of the cocoon of his fables and his myths. Perhaps it was the ominous political climate. Even Schulz could not remain impervious to it, though there is surprisingly little evidence of it in his letters and his writings. He alludes to the *Anschluss* in nearby Austria only once, as a "shattering historical event," and occasionally he voices his fear of losing his job, presumably owing to the rise of anti-Semitism in Poland. Yet nowhere do we find any indication that he thought about historical things deeply, or that he tried to evaluate them from a moral standpoint. It sometimes seems that he had no opinions at all, only metaphors, visions, fantasies.

When, as a consequence of the secret protocol of the Ribbentrop-Molotov Pact, Drohobycz was occupied by the Soviets, he took up a job as a decorator for official communist party functions. Schulzologists still quarrel about whether he did or did not paint portraits of Stalin. He timidly complained about the aesthetic concessions he was forced to make, and in one letter he regretted his "lack of elasticity and a refusal to compromise." Then came the Nazis, the ghetto, and his horrifying servile "relationship" with Hauptscharführer Felix Landau, one of the murderers of Drohobycz's Jews. This was another sort of abjection. To be sure, Schulz, like so many others, was fighting for survival, and the history of the Holocaust holds many equally strange and fateful choices. But if they were choices, acts of will, then one would hope to find traces of his thinking about his predicament in some of his writings, or at least in fragments of remembered conversations.

Witnesses told Ficowski that in this last period Schulz spoke about writing a chronicle of the martyrdom of the Jews. He was alleged even to have made notes for such a work, but nothing of those notes remains, and the silence surrounding his final months is excruciating. One of the last images of Schulz recorded by Ficowski shows him lying on his back on a scaffolding, like Michelangelo in the Sistine Chapel, painting frescoes on the ceiling in the Gestapo offices in Drohobycz. What was he thinking about? Was the chrysalis finally broken? Was he a helpless insect, naked in the storm that was about to crush him and his world? or was he thinking only about the empty wall to be covered with faces, shapes, visions, the "exuberant mildew" that seemed to hold the promise of "limitless possibilities of being"? We shall never know, and it is hard to tell which of the alternatives is more terrible to contemplate.

East European writers, we are told, have been often cast by history in the role, to paraphrase Shelley, of moral legislators of their people. They were supposed to stand like immovable rocks in the turbulent sea of their region's fate. On a closer look, however, they appear, with a few notable exceptions, to be a strangely mercurial and unstable lot. It is not uncommon to see the same defender of absolute truths transform himself over the years from a devout Catholic into a zealous Stalinist, a dissenting Marxist, a leftist liberal, a free-market libertarian, a communitarian conservative, and back into a devoted Catholic — all the while insisting upon an aura of uncompromising moral authority.

From his first literary attempts in the late 1920s until his death in 1969, Witold Gombrowicz, who spent most of his life in Argentina, not only avoided those strange intellectual per-mutations, but also offered a rather plausible explanation of the East European phenomenon in his own radical philosophy of endlessly shifting, transforming selfhood. In his three-volume *Diary*, considered by many his most accomplished work, Gom-browicz advanced a theory that Polish writers are individuals only in a superficial sense.[1] They are, in fact, social institutions "inhibited by something impersonal, superior, inter-human and collective emanating from the milieu. . . . Polish thought,

Polish mythology, the Polish psyche." Overwhelmed by their sense of importance and duty, they almost never feel free to develop their spirits and become masters of their imagination. In a country like Poland, suggested Gombrowicz, one does not become a writer to express something personal and authentic — a vision or an idea. One chooses the role of writer and then looks around for a vision or an idea that at a given moment serves the writer's Promethean task. As a result, those who selflessly devote themselves to some high communal ideal are likely to change that ideal with every turn of history. On the other hand, those who choose the path of self-centered individualism, like Gombrowicz himself, often turn out to be the most consistent and solid, as artists and as men. The self, even a transforming and capricious one, is a more powerful moral anchor, claimed Gombrowicz, than any abstract system imposed on the individual by the cultural milieu.

Gombrowicz built his literary reputation on many such paradoxes. He was a Polish writer who did not care much for Polish literature, a modernist who derided most of the major currents of modernity, and a skeptical, ironic mind with deep moralistic inclinations. In the 1970s some critics tried to present him as a forerunner of postmodernism, but in his own time he did not fit into any category.

He was born in 1904 into a family of affluent landed gentry, but in his youth he was afraid of dogs and horses, which pretty much disqualified him as a country squire. At school he distinguished himself in Polish and French, failing most other subjects. He studied law at Warsaw University, where he made his valet attend some of the less enthralling courses. Later he was sent by his family to continue his education at the Institut des Hautes Etudes Internationales in Paris. After a year, however, his father ended his allowance, adducing his son's "disorderly life" and the bad company he kept. Reluctant to return to Poland, Gombrowicz left for the Pyrenees, where he apparently got into trouble with the police and was rescued by a priest, who became a close friend. Eventually he returned to Poland, and in order to regain his family's support he accepted a clerical position at the Warsaw court.

By his own description, in a long conversation with Dominique de Roux published in English as *A Kind of Testament* (1973), Gombrowicz was living a triple life: as a country gentleman and a mother's darling, arrogant and naive; as a budding intellectual who wanted to be a writer (but not that much, as he admits); and as something he could not properly define but that appeared morbid, repugnant, and fascinating at the same time.[2] "I was abnormal, twisted, degenerate, abominable, and solitary," he said. "I slunk along, hugging the walls. Where could I find this secret blemish, which separated me from the human heart?"

Such confessions may be read perhaps as self-dramatizations of his early illicit sexual impulses that led him on embarrassing escapades to servants' quarters on his father's estate and to lumpen proletarian neighborhoods in Warsaw. But Gombrowicz approached his private torments seriously and intellectually. While looking for the secret blemish that apparently made him less complete and mature than others, he discovered that human beings in general are less mature, less complete, less defined, even less human than they would have liked to believe. Man appeared to him as constantly below the level of his own consciousness and culture, yet also unable to exist outside appearances.

Gombrowicz explored this subject in his early collection of surreal short stories titled *Memoirs of a Time of Immaturity* (1933), later retitled *Bacacay,* and in his first novel, *Ferdydurke* (1937), in which a thirty-year-old writer bearing resemblance to Gombrowicz is kidnapped by an elderly professor and forced to relive his years as a high school student.[3] The novel begins as a hilarious, pitiless satire on the inanities of school life, and during my own high school years it was a cult reading among young people — a kind of *Catcher in the Rye, Cat's Cradle,* and *Catch-22* rolled into one. But the novel soon takes a more sinister turn (without losing its comic quality) when the school is taken over by two rival student gangs — one espousing juvenile cynicism and smut, and the other youthful innocence and idealism, both fighting for the body and soul of a clumsy, hapless boy whom the cynics want to teach "the facts of life," if necessary by force.

Gombrowicz said that the puerile farce was meant as a retort to his detractors, who saw him as an immature writer (instead of a writer of immaturity) and often sent him "back to school." "But my words were soon whirled away in a violent dance, they took the bit between their teeth and galloped towards a grotesque lunacy with such speed that I had to rewrite the first part of the book in order to give it the same grotesque intensity." After his school adventure the kidnapped protagonist of *Ferdydurke* is made to lodge with a pompous "progressive" family whose liberated teenage daughter is simultaneously tempting a young stag and enticing the worshipful adulations of an elderly professor. Acting on a whim, the protagonist arranges a *ménage à trois* during which the studied progressive persona of the girl is crushed under the simultaneous, clashing assault of the lust of the youngster and the worship of the elder.

After the scandalous, voyeuristic prank the protagonist escapes to a country manor — in Polish culture a frequent symbol of traditional values and rural gentility — where another sexual intrigue triggers a social revolution and apparently brings down the quaint, patriarchal order of the country estate.

As the bizarre, increasingly fantastic plot of the novel unfolds, it becomes clear that the book not only mocks the venerable social institutions of school, family, and country life, but also throws into relief the incessant role acting that human beings engage in as they desperately try to assure themselves and others that they really inhabit their supposedly whole, finished, mature selves.

Gombrowicz the narrator seems somehow surprised by this unexpected discovery of the way in which the deep-rooted anxiety of his characters about their selves and their maturity turns into something independent, external, uncontrollable, ominous, and ridiculous at the same time. As if to explore the possibilities hidden in this discovery, he suspends the narrative of the novel right after the schoolroom episode to tell a seemingly unrelated story titled "The Child Runs Deep in Filidor," in which two illustrious scholars — a professor of High Synthesis and his colleague, a High Analyst — are gradually reduced to childishness while trying to prove the advantages of their respective philosophical methods.

The story is preceded by a preface in which the author explains what he sees as the fundamental predicament of humanity:

I don't know, truly, whether such things should pass my lips this day, but the stipulation — that an individual is well defined, immutable in his ideas, absolute in his pronouncements, unwavering in his ideology, firm in his tastes, responsible for his words and deeds, fixed once and for all in his ways — is flawed. Consider more closely the chimerical nature of such a stipulation. Our element is unending immaturity. What we think, feel today will unavoidably be silliness to our great-grandchildren. It is better that we should acknowledge today that portion of silliness that time will reveal . . . and the force that impels you to a premature definition is not, as you think, a totally human force. We shall soon realize that the most important is not: to die for ideas, styles, theses, slogans, beliefs; and also not: to solidify and enclose ourselves in them; but something different, it is this: to step back a pace and secure a distance from everything that unendingly happens to us.

The theory of inherent, deeply concealed "silliness" all of us carry within ourselves and invariably succumb to, especially in circumstances that call for displays of solemnity and astuteness, will become the principal motif of Gombrowicz's writing and the staple of the whole Gombrowiczean approach to man, history, and culture.

But the "silliness" and "immaturity" that modern man discovers in himself have for the Polish author grave, often destructive consequences. Unsure of his inner constitution, seeking a foothold in the shifting psychological universe, man gropes for what Gombrowicz called form, a fictitious and unstable construct that man mistakes for his true, unique self.

In the preface to "The Child Runs Deep in Filidor," the author states,

> [A] human being does not express himself forthrightly and in keeping with his nature but always in some well-defined form, and this form, this style, this manner of being is not of our making but is thrust upon us from outside — and this is why one and the same individual can present himself on the outside as wise or stupid, as bloodthirsty or angelic, as mature or immature — depending upon the style he happens to come up with, and in what way he is dependent on others. And just as beetles, insects chase after food all day, so do we tirelessly pursue form, we hassle other people with our style, our manners while riding in a streetcar, while eating or enjoying ourselves, while resting or attending to our business — we always, unceasingly, seek form, and we delight in it or suffer by it, and we conform to it or we violate and demolish it, or we let it create us, amen.

And then he adds a warning that will return in many of his later works, especially in the eccentric *Diary* he kept during the later years of his life: "Oh, the power of Form! Nations die because of it. It is the cause of wars. It creates something in us that is not of us. If you make light of it you'll never understand stupidity nor evil nor crime."

Like most modernists, Gombrowicz believed that modern man, bereft of God and a clear sense of his own identity, must constantly conceive himself, or be conceived, out of nothingness. Unlike most other modernists, however, he saw this process neither as a lonely effort of the autonomous human will, nor as a work of anonymous social forces. In his *Diary*, Gombrowicz wrote, "I do not deny that the individual is dependent on his milieu—but for me it is far more important, artistically far more creative, psychologically far more profound and philosophically far more disturbing that man is also created by an individual man, by another person. In chance encounters. Every minute of the day."

Man, claimed Gombrowicz, exists only in relation to other men. When left alone he is a shapeless, changeable lump of contradictions. He receives Form—his self, his character, his multiple public images—in myriads of encounters with others. The persona by which he knows himself and is known to the world is defined not within an individual, but in the interhuman space that Gombrowicz called the "inter-human church." The process is philosophically disturbing, says the writer, because no one really controls it—neither the individual nor the environment. Form appears "like a wave made up of a million tiny particles, which takes on a specific form every minute." Thus created, Form is often ridiculous and awkward. More importantly, however, it is the only thing modern man can hold on to when describing his identity. There is no authentic self that can be liberated from Form. Man is always artificial, and his rebellion inevitably turns into a new Form: "Form is not in harmony with the essence of life, but all thought which tries to describe this imperfection also becomes Form and thereby only confirms our striving for it."

What is more, the striving for Form often degenerates into aggressive posturing in front of someone considered inferior within a social or cultural system. In confessional passages of his *Diary* and in some interviews Gombrowicz indicated that he was made aware of this phenomenon by observing the rituals of his own social milieu, the Polish landowning gentry. He recalls, for example, a scene that appears in numerous variations in many of his works: "a farm-hand in a pea jacket, his head bare under the rain, talking to my brother Janusz, wearing a coat and sheltered under an umbrella. The hardness of the farm-hand's eyes, his cheeks, his mouth, in the pouring rain. . . . Beauty." The two human forms confronting each other — the master and the servant, the superior and the inferior — exist only in relation to each other. Each one without the other would be something else, a different configuration of "a million tiny particles."

After the publication of *Ferdydurke* Gombrowicz was finally admitted into the circle of young, avant-garde literati, where he became famous as an acerbic wit and self-appointed literary gadfly. Even he, however, could not predict that fate would soon place him in a situation as incongruous and bizarre as that of many of his protagonists and that his next novel, *Trans-Atlantyk*, arguably his most outlandish and fanciful work, would also be — after a fashion — his most personal and autobiographic one.

On the eve of World War II Gombrowicz was invited by the Polish government to take part in the maiden voyage of the ocean liner *Boleslaw Chrobry*. Together with another young writer he was to be paraded before the Polish community in Argentina as an "ambassador of Polish culture." It remains a mystery why the Polish government invited Gombrowicz to take part in this venture, and why the writer accepted the dubious assignment. Gombrowicz's irreverence toward national solemnities and his unconventional literary style, surreal and conceptual at once, made him a strange choice for a literary envoy to conservative Polish *estancieros* in Argentina. Besides, war was inevitable, and one would expect the Polish government to have had more important things on its mind.

Indeed, war broke out shortly after the *Chrobry* docked in Buenos Aires. Overcome by the absurdity of the situation and by the empty patriotic rhetoric of his travel companions, Gombrowicz decided to stay in Argentina rather than return to Europe. Yet the role of a wretched, forlorn émigré seemed to him all too Polish, and in order to extricate himself from this familiar costume he needed a radical gesture. "I felt anachronistic draped in an antique style, entangled in some sort of almost ancient scleroticism—and this cheered me up so much that I immediately commenced writing something that was to have been an antiquated memoir from that time," he recalled many years later. "In my position it was important to write something quickly which could be translated and published in foreign languages. Or, if I wanted to write something for the Poles, something which didn't injure their national pride."

Instead Gombrowicz produced a novel that was practically untranslatable and that went to great lengths to offend its Polish readers. "What a luxury I permitted myself in my misery!" marveled the author in an interview given near the end of his life. One has to commend the English translators of the book, Carolyn French and Nina Karsov, for tackling the challenge with daring and grace. For the challenge is considerable: the style of *Trans-Atlantyk* is a parody of the seventeenth-century Polish tale developed as an oral genre by the Polish gentry. Later on it acquired the status of the style most representative of the worst and the best features of the Polish mentality as it was envisioned by the Romantic mythmakers. This style, boastful and hyperbolic, full of bizarre neologisms and grammatical monstrosities, was said to convey the rugged pastoral chivalry, the verbal jingoism, and the drunken fantasy of provincial Polish squires. The original Polish tales from that time were usually fantastic narratives about military exploits or, like Gombrowicz's novel, picaresque stories about travels to remote and fantastic lands.

The translators point out that, in their search for an English equivalent, they reached for the language of Samuel Pepys and the lesser English prose writers of the seventeenth and eighteenth centuries. The result is a highly inventive linguistic mixture that conveys much of the energy and self-parody of the original. Through no fault of the translators, however, it lacks the rich historical associations and the literary references of Gombrowicz's work. This is unfortunate because most of the novel's meaning is conveyed through the particular resonance of its language. Retold in uncontemporary English, the episodes of the story may sound too much like the antiquated farce they were supposed to mock.

In one of the opening scenes, reminiscent of Joseph Conrad's *Lord Jim*, the protagonist, who bears Gombrowicz's name, sneaks down the gangway of a ship—the symbolic Polish ship of state—departing from Argentina to Poland. With evident relief, he inveighs against its martyred motherland: "Sail, sail, you Compatriots, to your People! Sail to that holy Nation of yours haply Cursed! Sail to that St. Monster Dark, dying for ages yet unable to die! Sail to your St. Freak, cursed by all Nature, ever being born and still Unborn! Sail, sail, so he will not suffer you to Live or Die but will keep you forever between Being and Non-being. Sail to your St. Slug that she may ever the more Enslime you."

Soon afterward, however, the protagonist falls into the snare set by a group of Argentinean Poles who inflate his literary reputation and set him up for a verbal duel with a local literary celebrity (in whom some detect the features of Jorge Luis Borges), supposedly in order to win respect for their country's artistic genius: "And here Pyckal and the Baron into my ear: 'Yoicks, yoicks!' Likewise the Counselor from the other side: 'Yoicks, yoicks, sick him, yoicks!' Say I: 'I am not a dog.' Whispered the Counsellor: 'Sick him, else Shame for he is their most Famous Author and it cannot be that they Celebrate him when the Great Polish Author, Genius is in the room! Bite him, you chitsht, you genius, bite him for if not, we will bite you!'"

This is only the first of many humiliations that befall the bemused hero. No sooner does he manage to elude his literary persecutors than he gets entangled in a bizarre tug-of-war between Colonel Tomasz, a noble Polish gentleman, and Gonzalo, a rich Argentinean homosexual who has set his eyes on Tomasz's young son Ignac. Forced to serve as a procurer, a false friend, and a second in a duel, the protagonist is torn between "Patria," the conservative, patriotic, and authoritarian world of the father, and "Filistria," the anarchic, morally ambiguous, and exciting kingdom of sons, into which Gonzalo tries to lure the innocent Ignac.

As in most novels and dramas by Gombrowicz, the battle for the hero's soul is fought by proxy as a battle for the body of a younger, immature, and often supposedly inferior person.

Soon the novelistic Gombrowicz discovers that Tomasz, in order to remove the stain of his son's seduction on his Polish honor, designs to kill Ignac with his own hands. At the same time Gonzalo wants to incite Ignac to kill his father. The plot grows even more fantastic when the hero is kidnapped and forcefully initiated into a secret society called the Order of the Chevaliers of the Spur, which in order to shock their compatriots into even greater patriotic frenzy is plotting to assassinate the Polish ambassador in Buenos Aires.

All this would be more than sufficient material for a farce about the phantasmagoric, insecure world of an émigré and about the Polish proclivity for self-aggrandizement, especially in a time of defeat. Yet the archaic, stylized language of the novel adds a strangely hollow and ominous resonance to the narratives. Its characters resemble miscast actors who use only the most conventional of gestures and rhetoric. Emptiness is the novel's predominant theme. The duel between Tomasz and Gonzalo is fought with empty pistols. Gonzalo's magnificent mansion, though filled with treasures, emanates vacancy and banality. The secret society was created out of a sense of emptiness by a humble accountant. "Empty, empty, empty" is the refrain repeated by the protagonist whenever he is called upon to take a moral stance. In the final scene of the novel, the emptiness erupts in a sudden burst of laughter that overpowers the characters and, happily, foils all their murderous plans. Yet the ending seems itself rather empty and inconclusive, as if the writer decided to walk away from his subject instead of striving for some kind of resolution.

Gombrowicz admitted in an interview that one of the aims of

the novel was to explode the "Polish legends" and to provoke his compatriots who were living among "chimeras, illusions, phraseology." While in Argentina he was irked by a tendency to turn the Polish tragedy into a political and moral cliché. He once remarked that Poland's problem was less that of "bad press" than of "bad poetry." He was also disturbed by his compatriots' willingness to perpetuate this lachrymose style and constantly to invoke the names of Copernicus, Chopin, and Kosciuszko as a claim to the world's sympathy and support. Gombrowicz believed that such behavior was embarrassing and counterproductive. He insisted that the true liberation of Poland should start with the liberation of the Polish spirit, which required a deliberately crass and provocative gesture: "Like a burst of laughter at a funeral."

And yet, a careful reader will notice that Gombrowicz's contentious and convoluted relationship with his Polishness is merely another articulation of his lifelong obsession with form.

In *Trans-Atlantyk* the formal critical mass is produced by the "national identity" and the strange claims it often puts on the individual. Yet most of the characters in the novel — the Polish patriots, the literati, the conspirators, even the dandy Gonzalo — seem to be trapped inside several, often contradictory Forms. If there is a darker shadow lurking behind their seemingly comic exploits, it is probably because at the time *Trans-Atlantyk* was written Gombrowicz was even more aware that "nations die" when Form becomes a unifying principle in a mass society. In an interview published toward the end of his life, he observed, "I say with amazement how, with the war, Europe, particularly Central and Eastern Europe, entered a demoniacal period of formal mobilization. The Nazis and the Communists fashioned menacing, fanatical masks for themselves; the fabrication of faiths, enthusiasm and ideals resembled the fabrication of cannons and bombs. Blind obedience and blind faith had become essential, and not only in the barracks. People were artificially putting themselves into artificial states, and everything — even and above all, reality — had to be sacrificed in order to obtain strength."

In his Argentinean exile Gombrowicz quite possibly experienced the shocking truth of his times more deeply than he was ready to admit: the ideological and political lunacy of the twentieth century could not be adequately explained either by "objective" historical processes or by a primordial evil of human nature. In fact, it did not seem to have any explanation beyond the "artificial states" of the collective mind that appeared out of nowhere and obliterated individual conscience.

In his novels and dramas, however, Gombrowicz preferred to study the corruptive influence of Form — or rather, of Form mistaken for Reality — in the microcosm of individual chance encounters. He was particularly interested in situations in which an imperceptible distortion, a ripple in the process in which Form creates itself, causes a sudden groundswell of absurdity leading to catastrophic results. All it takes is a minute misstep, a gratuitous whim, a hardly noticeable offbeat gesture. In *Ferdydurke* it is a strange urge of one of the protagonists to be slapped in the face by an inferior peasant. In *Pornografia*, the second novel written by Gombrowicz in Argentina, it is a clash between the rigid, highly formalized norms of "honorable" behavior under Nazi occupation and the puerile sexual fantasies of one of the protagonists.[4] In the author's last novel, *Cosmos*, it is an obsessive need to find a connection between a strangled bird discovered by a protagonist in a wood and a young married couple met in a mountain resort.[5] Family hierarchies, social conventions, rituals of love and courtship lead inadvertently to their self-negation in Gombrowicz's plays *The Marriage* and *Ivona, Princess of Burgundia*.[6] On the other hand, revolution — an apparent rebellion against inflexible form — relapses into its own formal rigidity in *Operetta*.[7]

Yet if there is no escape from Form, as Gombrowicz seemed to believe, how could tragedies be avoided? There is no clear answer to those questions in Gombrowicz's world. The only clue is the burst of laughter at the end of *Trans-Atlantyk*. In order to save oneself from the dictatorship of Form, he seems to suggest, modern man has to learn to treat his own ideas, his art, his political doctrines a little bit less seriously. He needs to become aware of the artificiality of all Great Ideas, especially when they compel one to Great Deeds. Only in this way can he transform himself from someone who has Form into someone who creates Form. In 1954, he wrote in his *Diary*, "To be a concrete man. To be an individual. Not to strive to transform the whole world. To live in the world, changing it only as much as possible from within the reach of my nature. To become real in harmony with my needs, my individual needs. I do not want to say that collective and abstract thought, that Humanity as such, are not important. Yet a certain balance must be restored. The most modern direction of thought is one that will re-discover the individual man."

Gombrowicz was clearly looking for a style that would

allow a more natural and free attitude toward culture, politics, and society:

> There exist two contrary types of humanism: one, which we could call the religious, tries to send man to his knees before a work of human culture — it forces us to adore and respect Music or Poetry, for example, or the State or Divinity; and the other, a more difficult current of our spirit which strives to restore man's sovereignty and independence in relation to the Gods and Muses, which are ultimately man's creation. In the second instance, the word "art" is written with a small letter. And it is beyond doubt that a style that is capable of encompassing both of these tendencies is fuller, more authentic, and more closely reflects the antinomies of our nature than a style that expresses only one of these two poles of our emotions.

Gombrowicz saw his "philosophy of form" as an attempt to demystify man, to reveal the hidden paradoxes that govern his existence, to strip him of his cultural fetishes, and to replace them with what he called "the difficult childhood of an adult": "First, push away all the things that made everything easier, find yourself in a cosmos that is as bottomless as you can stand, in a cosmos at the limits of your consciousness, and experience a condition where you are left to your own loneliness and your own strength, only then, when the abyss which you have not managed to tame throws you from the saddle, sit down on the earth and discover the sand and grass anew."

That venture inevitably made Gombrowicz confront two contemporary philosophies that also presented the demystification of consciousness as their main goal, Marxism and existentialism. In the *Diary*, the author describes his relationship with existentialism as "tormentingly unclear and tense. It intrudes into my existence, but I don't want it. And it is not I who am in this predicament. Strange. Philosophy, exhorting to authenticity, leads us into gigantic falsehoods." Gombrowicz notes the existentialist message of his first novel, *Ferdydurke*, in which the protagonist's peregrinations and his incessant, unwitting role acting represent, according to the author, "existence in a vacuum, nothing except existence."

Yet at the same time Gombrowicz rejects the existentialist concept of the absolute moral freedom of an individual. In his remarks on Albert Camus' *The Rebel*, he says, "Conscience, the individual conscience, does not have the power that it has for [Camus] as far as saving the world. Don't we see again and again that conscience has almost no voice in the matter? Does man kill or torture because he has come to the conclusion that he has the right to do so? He kills because others kill. He tortures because others torture. The most abhorrent deed becomes easy if the road to it has been paved, and, for example, in concentration camps the road to death was so well trodden that the bourgeois incapable of killing a fly at home exterminated people with ease."

This insistence that it is not the individual consciousness, but its relationship with others, that dictates moral and existential choice — that man is merely a theoretical concept apart from the social context — brought Gombrowicz dangerously close to Marxism, which also postulated that man is a historical product of social and economic conditions. Gombrowicz was aware of this proximity and its implications. His *Diary* displays a great deal of intellectual effort to clarify both his intellectual attraction to communism and his instinctive rejection of it. He starts by dismissing what he considered the wrong, or sentimental, reasons for the rejection of communism: love of the past, God as an absolute justification of a particular order, a common pity for the victims of revolutionary upheavals. "Communism can be judged effectively," he says, "only from the perspective of the most severe and profound sense of existence, never from a point of view that is superficial and subdued, never from a bourgeois point of view." He decided to test the communist dialectic against itself, to show that the communist dialectic is not quite dialectic enough. It is a dirty trick, he concludes, a fraud meant to trap the critical mind.

Communist dialectics, that hard, surgical tool so capable at dissecting, unmasking, and demystifying the "fetishes" and the contradictions of the old world, suddenly lost its legitimacy, Gombrowicz caustically observes, within communism's own precincts: "I am allowed to cast aspersion on my own truths as long as I am on the side of capitalism, but this same self-checking is supposed to cease the minute I join the ranks of the revolution. Here dialectics suddenly gives way to dogma as a result of some astounding about-face. . . . And we see that we are once again confronted with one of the great mystifications, similar to those unmasked by Nietzsche, Marx, Freud, who revealed that behind the facade of our Christian, bourgeois, and sublimated morality vied other, anonymous, and brutal forces. Here the mystification is all the more perverse, however, in that it relies precisely on unmasking."

There was, perhaps, still another reason for Gombrowicz's rejection of communism. It appeared to him as one of the most extreme products of the modern mind that found itself alone within the world and tried to take control of it by the sheer effort of intellect. Perhaps the only true modernist in Polish letters, Gombrowicz did not believe enough in the power of thought to allow it to "tear into the world." The world should be allowed, instead, to create itself. "In this second instance the mind no longer asks what the world is supposed to be like and, instead, after narrowing its field of vision, asks, how am I to act in the world? The mind then becomes that which it has been for centuries: an instrument of individual cognition within the scale of a single life. In this reduced scale it feels surer of itself."

Gombrowicz's message of radical skepticism and individualism, combined with his iconoclasm, made him anathema among émigré Poles, with the exception of the Paris *Kultura* circle, but it met with a surprisingly positive response among the young, postwar intelligentsia in Poland, where some of his works started to be available after the thaw of 1956. His prewar fiction, *Trans-Atlantyk* and *Bacacay*, was published officially, and his dramas—*Ivona*, *Operetta*, and *The Marriage*—were occasionally staged in Polish theaters. His later novels, *Cosmos* and *Pornografia*, and, most important, his *Diary* remained "unprintable" until the last years of communism, and even then they appeared in editions expurgated of any references to communism and the Soviet Union. Only after 1989, under the first democratically elected Polish government, were they restored to their original form.

But even truncated and censored Gombrowicz was a cultural icon among freethinking Polish intelligentsia. A writer who sneered at the role of a "committed" intellectual as "too pretentious and too frivolous" became, paradoxically, one of the mentors of the dissenting intellectuals of the sixties and seventies. Gombrowicz was a perfect antidote to the nationalist pieties dominant among the more conservative Polish opponents of communism. He cautioned against the dangers of excessive loyalty to the East European heritage of doom. He demonstrated that repeated historical disasters have hampered the spiritual development of the region and made the intellectual classes too self-conscious to be really creative and to achieve the spiritual freedom necessary to oppose collectivist doctrines.

This attitude, together with Gombrowicz's famous egotism and his disdain for literary idols (he considered Borges "unintelligent" and Marcel Proust "full of faults" and even tried to show that Dante's tercets could have been better written), made him delightfully subversive and liberating, especially in the stifling years of decaying communism. In retrospect, however, this iconoclast and intellectual rogue appears to be almost an apostle of normalcy and moderation. The rediscovery of the individual, the counsel of restraint in national self-adulation, the priority of concrete tasks over abstract ideals: all this sounds like a rather reasonable, albeit rarely followed, program for his still struggling native Eastern Europe.

Most of all, however, he was a great chastiser of Polish thinking classes: "A Pole does not know how to act toward Poland, it confuses him and makes him mannered. Poland inhibits the Pole to such a degree that nothing really 'works' for him. Poland forces him into a cramped state — he wants to help it too much, he wants to elevate it too much. . . . There is something here with which [Poles] are not yet comfortable."

If a Pole really wants to help Poland, claimed Gombrowicz, if he wants to make Poland equal to Europe, he should first become an authentic individual, that is, he should unlearn the habit of falling to his knees before Poland or Europe. He should first be capable of totally disregarding any form that is not uniquely his own. If Poland appears to be culturally immature, moreover, its very immaturity should become its trump card. A Pole, or any representative of a "secondary culture," should appear in a Western salon neither in a folk costume nor in a frock coat, but as someone "in between": formless, unkempt, unfinished. Only in this way can he save his freedom and prove that Europe, too, is less mature and less rooted in itself than it wants to appear.

In Gombrowicz's case, the strategy proved partly successful. In the late 1950s, owing to the efforts of his friend and promoter Konstanty Jelenski, a Polish writer living in Paris, his works started to appear in French translation and were favorably received. Jean-Paul Sartre credited him with the invention of the "new analytical novel." Publishers and critics in other countries also started to take an interest. At the end of his life, his name made the short list for the Nobel Prize: legend has it that he lost the prize in 1968 to Yasunari Kawabata by one vote.

Gombrowicz was deeply convinced that his discovery of the "drama of form" touched on some of the most crucial problems of modernity. Yet he remained an oddity, a maverick watched and admired from a distance: a Polish writer at war with Polish literature, a self-proclaimed European who held Europe in disdain, a critic of modern culture who had to pay to have his works translated. In his own time he became one of the very few Polish writers with a truly international career. But he was also living proof that the best works of "secondary cultures" usually see the light of day as artifacts of cultural archaeology. Still, in the *Diary*, his relative obscurity became a liberating force, giving the book its unique momentum and its intellectual boldness. Gombrowicz once pondered the aggressiveness of his "self" as it was set free on the pages of his journal and concluded, "Was it not because this 'self' living on the other side of the ocean was so insignificant, so marginal, so anonymous? I had nothing to lose. I could write whatever passed through my head—nobody cared. . . . I was nothing, so I could do anything."

At the beginning of Stanislaw Ignacy Witkiewicz's mad, surreal Bildungsroman *Insatiability*, first published in 1930 in Poland, a young Polish gentleman named Genezip Kapen, a sensitive high school graduate and the son of a brewer in the Carpathian region, looks into the starlit sky and is seized by a sense of cosmic melancholy: "Eternity was as nothing compared to the monstrous infinitude of time within infinite space and the heavenly bodies inhabiting it. What to make of the thing? It was beyond imagining and yet impressed itself on the mind with absolute ontological necessity."[1] As his aloof, tyrannical father lies dying, Genezip senses "something painfully sweet in this sensation of loneliness," and, running from his father's bedside, he sets out on a frenzied sexual and philosophical quest of self-discovery. He engages in a series of heated debates on art, love, being, science, theosophy, and religion with an assortment of characters, including a homosexual composer of cacophonous music, an avant-garde writer, a professor of symbolic logic, and an impoverished aristocrat turned neo-Catholic philosopher. Genezip is briefly seduced by the composer, but he ends the night in the arms of the mysterious and alluring Princess Irina, who is much advanced in years.

The erotic and the philosophical freely intermingle in the novel, and endless intellectualizing seems the favorite form of foreplay for the book's characters. In Irina's bed, Genezip muses, "The property of arbitrariness is immediately posited for every animate creature: it is an elementary fact of existence; under certain circumstances resistance engenders a feeling of limitation and relative necessity, whereas absolute necessity, because of the abstract elimination that occurs at the periphery of Particular Being or of living creatures in general, is *necessarily* a fiction." Young Zip, as he is also called, is growing up fast. In the course of the book's many pages we see him humiliated and rejected by Irina, joining a military school, reconciled with Irina, worshiping another fiendish, sadistic woman and murdering her gay chaperone, taking part in an aborted coup, and finally marrying an angelic beauty whom he strangles on their wedding night.

In the meantime, the whole world is imploding around Genezip and his companions. Western Europe is ruled by an array of "soft," pragmatic totalitarian regimes that manage to keep their populations complacent and materially satiated through superior labor organization. History has reached its limits or perhaps is preparing for another mad leap. In any case, the word is out that "the white man had ceased to believe in the myth of infinite progress and now saw the wall of obstruction in himself and not in nature." But there is a hyperreactionary "White" revolution going on in Russia, while from the Far East a "living wall" of Chinese is approaching with the intention of interbreeding with the Europeans and starting a new, as yet undefined era in the history of humanity.

In the middle of those global upheavals, as always, lies Poland, governed by an enigmatic dictator, General Kotzmolochowicz, and a shadowy junta known as the Syndicate for National Salvation. True to its historical tradition, Poland is constantly allying itself and fighting with all its neighbors, while at the same time remaining "absolutely unswerving in its heroic defense of the idea of the nation" and determined "to be a bastion, a role which in her torpor she gladly assumed." Alas, the country's elites fall prey to a drug-induced New Age religion of Murty Bing that preaches the Mystery of Panexistence, Maximal Oneness, and Duo-Unity. At the decisive historical moment the general, apparently moved by a sudden humanitarian impulse, surrenders his invincible army to the Chinese and is ceremoniously beheaded by the enemy. At the end of the story Genezip, "by now a consummate lunatic, a mild automaton," is forced to marry a beautiful Chinese princess and become a faithful servant of his new autocratic masters.

This bizarre book is set in a fantastic present played out in the costumes of interwar Poland. An innocent reader could be persuaded that he is reading a wordy, overdone, sometimes delightful parody of a generic Great Central European Novel, dense with murky eroticism, abstract cerebrations, and a general, almost comforting premonition of the impending end of history. The character of Kotzmolochowicz, a stable boy turned Maximum Leader and "the most unpredictable demon from among the intrepid souls still roaming about on the vanishing horizon of individualism," was probably modeled on Marshall Jozef Pilsudski, Poland's colorful, charismatic interwar leader, but he also bears resemblance to a more contemporary version of the Polish man of providence, Lech Walesa. His genius, it seems, consists mainly in his absolute cluelessness about everything that happens around him, so his erratic decisions befuddle his allies and enemies alike.

Insatiability, however, is not a parody. It is the real thing and one of the classics of European modernism. Its author (also called Witkacy, to distinguish him from his equally famous father, the Polish art critic Stanislaw Witkiewicz) is usually mentioned together with the two other literary innovators of his time, Bruno Schulz and Witold Gombrowicz. Something like a literary cult has grown up around the Three Madmen, as Gombrowicz used to call them. It is tempting to treat them almost as a single phenomenon. Together they thoroughly revolutionized Poland's literary sensibility after World War I and helped to place their country on the literary map of the modern world. They also displayed striking similarities in their lives as well as in their art. All three grappled with serious personal problems rooted in their family backgrounds and probably also in their disquieting, illicit sexual longings. They desired friendship but often turned it away by their impossible demands and idiosyncrasies. They were all obsessed with the question of form in art and with the incongruences of human relations.

Still, they are not quite as similar as critics and historians often make them seem. They did face similar dilemmas but each tried to resolve them in a radically different way. They also occupy quite distinct places in the history of modern letters. Schulz, probably the most gifted prose writer of the three, dazzles with his language and his imagination; he transformed the world of a Jewish Galician town, Drohobycz, into an enchanted, mythical domain. Gombrowicz continues to fascinate as the author of dreamlike dramas and as a thinker of striking originality. But Witkiewicz, the oldest of the trio, still baffles interpreters of his writing and his life. Was he a "metaphysical dandy" (Gombrowicz's term) and an epigone of nineteenth-century decadence? or a forerunner of today's radical irony? or was he, like the hero of *Insatiability*, a lunatic slowly sinking into incoherence?

Born in 1885 in Warsaw, Witkiewicz soon moved with his parents to the Carpathian village of Zakopane, which at the turn of the century was becoming a fashionable colony of Polish artists and intellectuals from nearby Krakow. His father, who, among his many pursuits, translated Leo Tolstoy into the dialect of Polish highlanders and invented an architectural style of elegant wooden chalets inspired by the peasant huts of the local mountain folk, educated his son at home. The young man grew up in the intense climate of turn-of-the-century bohemian life, soaking up arcane philosophical debates and what he called the demonic atmosphere of the entrancing mountain landscapes. Fluent in several languages, he later traveled to Italy, Germany, and France and studied at the Academy of Fine Art in Krakow. He lived through a tempestuous romance with a famous actress and the suicide of another great love. Distressed and on the brink of insanity, he joined his friend the anthropologist Bronislaw Malinowski on an expedition to Australia and New Guinea. They quarreled, allegedly about the interpretation of ethnographic data, and with the outbreak of World War I Witkiewicz sailed to St. Petersburg, where he joined the tsarist army as an officer in an elite infantry regiment.

In Russia he discovered his two lifelong passions: philosophy and hallucinatory drugs. Records indicate that he was fearless in battle — he received the Order of St. Anne for his courage — and that he was kind to his soldiers, who with the outbreak of the Bolshevik revolution of 1917 elected him their commissar. At this point, however, he decided to come home. He sneaked back to Poland and settled in Zakopane. He wrote philosophical tracts, plays, and novels; he painted and experimented with drugs (he can be credited with the invention of "psychedelic" art); and he participated in several avant-garde movements. He quickly gained notoriety, but a literary reputation was slow in coming.

Reconstituted after World War I as an independent state, Poland was, like most of East-Central Europe, a hotbed of modernist ideas and forms. Schools, styles, and sensibilities germinated at a frightening rate, as if driven by a sense of their own impermanence. It was a Dostoevskian world in which the educated classes took Great Ideas a bit too seriously for their own good. It was also a world teetering on the edge of destruction. The awakened nationalisms and extremist ideologies did not portend stability. The unfinished Great European War (also known as the War to End All Wars) was bracing for its second act. Historical catastrophism in the Europe of those days was an almost universal phenomenon, but in the eastern and central regions of the continent real catastrophes did happen with chilling regularity. It was in this world, at once euphoric and gloomy, that Witkiewicz settled into the role of its Dark Prince, a famous eccentric and scandal maker, worshiped by some and denounced by many as an imposter.

Witkiewicz was hardly an original or systematic thinker, but he treated his philosophy very seriously and conducted learned correspondence with several prominent philosophers of his time. Even today his body of philosophical writing, composed in a relentlessly oblique style, elicits committed, though often torturous, exegetic attempts. It is assumed that his numerous plays and his few novels were conceived mainly as case studies of his ontological, historical-philosophical, and aesthetic concepts. His worldview was built around the same metaphysical considerations that culminated in the "philosophy of existence" of Karl Jaspers, Martin Heidegger, and Jean-Paul Sartre. For Witkiewicz, the central property of human existence is strangeness. Our consciousness is constantly preoccupied with the question, Why? Why am I exactly this and not that being? At this point of ultimate space and in this moment of infinite time? In this group of beings, on this planet? Why do I exist, while I could have been without any existence? Why does anything exist at all? The mystery, the loneliness, and the frailty of being are the source of unbearable terror, yet terror is the only thing that makes us capable of higher strivings. Throughout history humankind has wrestled with the terror of being and turned it into the force of life — through religion, philosophy, and art. In the modern era of socialization, mechanization, and mass civilization, argued Witkiewicz, humankind has been deprived — or rather, deprived itself — of this vital source of creativity. It has discovered itself naked and in a metaphysical vacuum.

Like José Ortega y Gasset, Witkiewicz feared the political and cultural revolt of the masses that, in his view, would end all higher aspirations of humanity. The new civilization created by the mass man can make humanity superficially happy by tending to its material needs through progressive socialization of power, highly efficient organization of labor, technology, and social engineering. Yet this "happiness for all" can be achieved only through the surrender of the individual and the abandonment of the essentially disruptive, antisocial pursuit of metaphysical mysteries — that is, by making humans less human. It was the ominous shadow of Fyodor Dostoevsky's Grand Inquisitor that Witkiewicz, together with many other thinkers of the interwar era, saw hanging over the political landscape of his day. "From a herd we came," he wrote, " . . . and to a herd we shall return."

The last refuge of the individual, argues Witkiewicz, is art, which in the modern era tries to replace religion and philosophy by evoking metaphysical feelings. Art engages us through the unity of its structure, through Pure Form, rather than through ideas or mimetic representation. In order to play this role, art must defend its autonomy by transcending everyday experience and turning away from daily human concerns — from what Witkiewicz called "real-life feelings." To do so it must become maximally irrational, individualistic, deformed, and offensive to bourgeois tastes. Deformity, deviation, and the shocking quality of art, argued Witkiewicz, are necessary because art is "a kind of narcotic whose effect is to evoke what I have called metaphysical feeling through a grasp of formal construction." But the effect of narcotics weakens with use, and the addict craves ever-larger doses.

Witkiewicz admitted that Pure Form in art is merely a philosophical postulate and in practical terms artistic expression probably cannot do without some "real-life" element. Even in his paintings he did not advocate pure abstraction, and his favorite genre was bizarre, deformed portraiture.[2] In a lecture entitled "Pure Form in the Theater" he said that since art is created by real living people with real experience of material reality, art will always be directed, at least in part, at the external world: "Some sort of beings will always act and speak on the stage, parts of the compositions in paintings will always be more or less analogous to actual objects in the visible world, and the reason is the impossibility of dispensing with dynamic and directional tensions." But he stressed that imitation of life is art's "inessential element" and should not be allowed to assume the first place. What is essential is Pure Form, which, in Witkiewicz's view, should aspire to "metaphysical beauty" and imitate nothing except the very structure of Being—paradoxical, unexpected, and infinitely strange.[3]

Witkiewicz believed that in literature the dramatic form is most likely to approach the ideal of Pure Form because the text is only one of several structural components. Theater seemed to offer the possibility of highly complex "formal ordering and composition" without much concern for meaning in the traditional sense, "so that onstage a human being, or some other creature, could commit suicide because of the spilling of a glass of water, after having five minutes before danced with joy on account of his dearly beloved mother's death; so that a little five-year-old girl could give a lecture on [Karl Friedrich] Gauss's coordinates for apelike monsters beating gongs and constantly chanting the word *kalafar*."

Witkiewicz wrote over thirty plays according to this abstract formalist principle. The majority of them were never published, let alone staged, during his lifetime. They were discovered and published in a single volume in the early 1960s, when Polish literature was breaking out of its socialist-realist corset and taking a new interest in its modernist roots. (Schulz and Gombrowicz also made their Polish reappearance around that time, though Gombrowicz only selectively, since his politics were unpalatable to the communist authorities.)

Many of Witkiewicz's dramas are available in English in splendid translation and with perceptive critical commentary by Daniel Gerould, one of the best contemporary Witkiewicz scholars.[4] All of them share an aura of absurdity, and their plots are deliberately inconsistent. Their personae sometimes appear to be real characters, sometimes participants in some grotesque, slightly wicked party game, and sometimes they are clearly unsure of their status or even doubt their existence.

In his departure from realism Witkacy probably went further than Luigi Pirandello or Gombrowicz. His dramas are rightly considered harbingers of Samuel Beckett, Eugene Ionesco, and the Theater of the Absurd. "When leaving the theater," he wrote in one of his programmatic essays, "one should have the impression that one wakes up from a strange dream, in which the most trite things have the elusive, deep charm characteristic of dreams, not comparable to anything." But several of those plays also contain discernable references to social and political realities. Among the most often staged are "Shoemakers," which can be read as a meditation on the "revolt of the masses," and "The Crazy Locomotive," usually interpreted as an allegory of machine-driven, out-of-control industrial civilization. The author's favorite plotlines—if that is what they are—concern dysfunctional families or elaborate sexual *ménages* set against the backdrop of some indefinite social calamity or revolution. Under the guise of Pure Form there simmers a perplexing brew of the author's ideas and private obsessions: metaphysical longings, catastrophist visions, sexual fixation and morbidity, with an occasional additive of political satire.

An even stranger mixture of elements can be found in Witkiewicz's four known novels, *The 622 Downfalls of Bungo, or The Demonic Woman* (written around 1911 but not published until 1972), *The Only Way Out* (discovered and published in 1968), *Farewell to Autumn*[5] (1927), and *Insatiability*—all sharing the subject of a mad individualist-artist-philosopher at the end of time, when the world sinks first into chaos and then into spiritual torpor. The writer refused to grant the novel the status of art, considering it a mixed-breed form organically incapable of achieving higher structural unity. As a novelist, therefore, he allowed himself more freedom in dealing with his ideas and his preoccupations. For this reason, Witkiewicz's novels are often interpreted as extravagant novels of ideas. According to this approach, *Insatiability* should be read as the story of a young man "suffused with the fiery essence of life's weirdness," trying to affirm his identity and to find an answer to his metaphysical why in a world in which all the lights—religious, philosophical, artistic—are dimming and dying. The novel has also been hailed as a Polish version of *Brave New World* or *1984*, a dark prophecy of the destruction of the individual and the advent of totalitarianism, a warning that was to be fulfilled a mere nine years later.

And yet it is impossible to take *Insatiability* seriously as an exploration of philosophical or political ideas. Among the novel's surreal imagery and mad narrative twists there is precious little room for coherent thought. The book's endless pseudo-philosophical elucidations seem to collapse under their own weight or peter out in an adolescent whimper: "Can *this* be me, is this *my* life unfolding"; or, "Why out of a billion possibilities *this* way and not some other way? Oh, God!" The author's sexual phobias become uncomfortably obvious, as the sex scenes grow gratuitously weird and the narrator takes evident pleasure in constantly thrashing the novel's women and calling them names. What is more, despite Zip's insatiable devouring of raw experience ("I keep wanting to touch everything naked, just as I touch my face with my own bare hand. . . . I want to change everything so it'll turn out as it should. I want to have it *all*, to choke it, to crush it, squeeze its guts out, torture it!") everything in the novel — people, situations, ideas — has the feel of cardboard artificiality.

The social and political message of the novel, if taken literally, is dubious at best and quite disturbing. Witkiewicz appears to be defending individualism, but he finds this virtue only among the aristocracy of the spirit, that is, among artists and madmen. And he finds it only in acts of transgression: "By that monstrous crime I liberated myself," Genezip proclaims, like a standard Nietzschean superman. As for ordinary people, they are presented as a "drab, colorless mass of languishing phantoms . . . heaving aimlessly about," as "superfluous minibrains," as a "consented machine," as "toiling apes." They are beyond hope. They need to be molded by Kotzmolochowicz's iron will or to blend into "a homogeneous and stuporous state."

Some Polish intellectuals of the sixties tried to construe Witkiewicz's dark vision as an indictment of communism and defense of liberal democratic values. But the author's praise of individualism has a clearly antidemocratic and antiliberal vector. It seems that instead of an ideological dictatorship, Witkiewicz sees the main threat to civilization in popular democracy driven by the pursuit of material, "consumerist" fulfillment and political equality. His charges against "automation," "socialization," and "rule of great numbers" may sound like a quarrel with Soviet-style communism, but in his day such expressions were usually employed against modern civilization in general, including the allegedly soulless, narrowly pragmatic bourgeois liberalism. In fact, argue Witkiewicz's characters, the decline started with the "vicious democratic lie born of the French Revolution" and culminated in the English industrial revolution: "It was they [the English] who established the greediest, most stultifying, most barbaric state, that built on money—an older version of America which, by its example, has reduced us to a state of sluggish manatees through its perfidious organization of labor."

In the years in which this novel was written, such sentiments, often mixed with millenarian despair and metaphysical "hunger for Being," pushed a legion of yearning souls from Vienna to Dublin into the embrace of extreme ideologies. In Witkiewicz's world, fascism and bolshevism are horrifying but inevitable and well-deserved products of Western civilization. By returning humanity to the state of a mindless herd ruled over by a few strong-willed, ruthless individuals, they seem to close one cycle of history and promise to start a new one. At least they titillate Genezip's aesthetic, quasi-metaphysical receptive organs. He feels queasy when he sees his father's brewery workers herded into their prisonlike living quarters, yet he finds "something erotic" in this spectacle of human degradation: "There they were now, a trailing column that stretched along the road that led from the factory compound to the manor in the pale azure dusk of a fading winter evening broken up by the violet sheaves of light given off by the arc lamps." Witkiewicz kept away from politics and never crossed the line transgressed by Ezra Pound, Knut Hamsun, Gabriele D'Annunzio, and numerous other modern aesthetes turned fascists or fascist sympathizers. And yet, his writing conveys some of the least appealing dispositions of the modernist sensibility.

Unless, of course, *Insatiability* is an immense joke played on that sensibility and on the inflamed literary culture that produced it. Witkiewicz's contemporaries did not detect such a satirical intention in his novel, but this is the direction in which the novel's translator, Louis Iribarne, a professor of Slavic languages and literatures at the University of Toronto, seems to be pointing when he says in an interview that the book is "set to bury itself and Western civilization which has given rise to it." Iribarne has translated *Insatiability* with unsurpassed linguistic inventiveness (and not once but twice, since he attempted it first as Czeslaw Milosz's student at Berkeley, with merely three years of Polish under his belt).[6] The parodical element in *Insatiability* is, in his view, unmistakable. How else should we treat sentences such as this: "His ego had collided with the totality of existence in an unutterable spasm, then with that miserable worm known as humanity"? Is Witkiewicz the novelist undermining Witkiewicz the philosopher and aesthete? Is he imply-

ing that metaphysical obsession may be not only the justification of existence, but also its deadly poison? The search for
metaphysical truths in modern times will bear no fruit, and it
will also ineluctably turn into self-mockery, into "metaphysical
masturbation," as Genezip has to admit. A novel that attempts
to describe such a search can only be a caricature of a novel,
a tortured and sometimes unreadable verbal mass embracing
everything yet signifying nothing.

It is an attractive interpretation, if only because granting
the novel a postmodern intention is about the only way of
saving it today. One should not exclude the possibility that
Witkiewicz possessed such a great ironic distance from his preoccupations. The problem is that those who knew Witkiewicz
testify that he treated himself with almost childish seriousness,
even when joking. He often surprised his friends by staging
crazy happenings at his Zakopane villa, productions involving
strange disguises and scatological props, and then he was dis-
appointed when his guests were actually amused. He wanted
them to be scandalized, horrified, or awed by the profundity of
his rebellion.

Perhaps Gombrowicz, who much preferred the humble,
awkward Schulz to the self-regarding, theatrical Witkiewicz,
was right when he said that Witkiewicz "ruined himself . . .
lured by his own demonism, and not knowing how to reconcile
the abnormal with the normal. Consequently, he was left at the
mercy of his eccentricity. All mannerisms result from the inability to oppose form, a certain manner of being rubs off on
us, becomes habit-forming." Gombrowicz noted elsewhere
that Witkiewicz's "human being is grotesque in his spasmodic

excitation at his own abyss." It is quite possible, too, that he used humor, self-mockery, theatrical grimaces, and irony less to undermine the message of his work than to exorcise his darker demons—the demons of the Central European universe and the more personal ones. For they were tearing at the fabric of his life and art.

These were the demons with which all of them, Gombrowicz, Schulz, and Witkiewicz, were struggling. But they struggled differently. Schulz shut himself up in his art and built, out of his language and his imagination, a cocoon of parallel reality. Gombrowicz rejected the "monstrousness of metaphysics" and chose to adopt an aristocratic, ironic detachment toward the human comedy. Witkiewicz tried to stare "metaphysical horror" in the face, yet hid behind the mask of a jester.

At the outbreak of the war he was seen walking east to escape the approaching troops of the Third Reich. Eyewitnesses claim he committed suicide on September 18, 1939, when he learned that Soviet troops had crossed the Polish border and were moving westward, thus seemingly confirming his dark end-of-history premonitions. Some time ago his admirers exhumed what they believed to be his roadside grave, so as to reinter his remains in a more appropriate place. The grave turned out to contain the skeleton of a young woman. Witkiewicz has vanished. It is tempting to imagine him still roaming about out there, the most distraught and the most enigmatic of the great East European madmen.

Nobody could tell the story of this age better than Czeslaw Milosz, the master of eccentric vision. He was born in 1911, and he had seen it all: genocidal wars, revolutions, whole countries violently erased or slowly fading from the map, the rise and ebb of ideologies, philosophies, religions. Growing up between the two world wars in the Lithuanian city of Vilnius, with its Polish and Lithuanian nationalisms and the long shadow of Soviet expansionism, Milosz joined a group of Marxist-leaning "catastrophist" poets, Zagary. Their visions of mass terror and annihilation, taken by their elders for a literary pose, were soon surpassed by reality. Later, in Nazi-occupied Warsaw, Milosz published in clandestine literary periodicals, wrote essays on the rise of modern sensibility, conducted a learned correspondence on the crisis of Christianity with his friend Jerzy Andrzejewski (both the wartime essays and the letters were published in English as *Legends of Modernity*), and translated Jacques Maritain, Shakespeare, and T. S. Eliot.[1]

After the war, Milosz spent his days in the diplomatic service of communist Poland but devoted his nights to writing a series of poems called "Daylight." Their mixture of moral seriousness and ironic distance became for Polish poets the standard idiom of dignity, a form of aesthetic resistance against the stream of official lies. One of the poems from this series, "You Who Have

Wronged," written in Washington in 1950, was later selected by Solidarity to be inscribed on the monument to Gdansk shipyard workers killed during the protests of 1970. Its classical form — in Polish it consists of two eleven-syllable quatrains, a tercet, and a couplet, linked by an intricate rhyming pattern — underscores its steel-cold message:

> Do not feel safe. The poet remembers.
> You kill one, but another is born
> The words are written down, the dead, the date.
> And you'd have done better with a morning dawn
> A rope, and a branch bowed beneath your weight.[2]

After breaking with the communists and emigrating to France in 1951, where he was accepted neither by the progressive French intellectuals nor by the conservative Polish émigrés, Milosz survived in monastic poverty and worked on what would become his best-known book of prose, *The Captive Mind*, a study of intellectual acquiescence in communism.[3] In 1961 he moved to California, where he accepted the professorship in Slavic literatures at the University of California in Berkeley and watched with curiosity the inanity of American consumerism and the budding youth counterculture. But there, too, he remained faithful to the "estate of Polish literature," claiming (in his case, a little exaggeratedly) that "communing outside a shared language, a shared history" is impossible.[4] A lifelong nomad and a perpetual stranger, Milosz seems addicted to looking at things from unordinary perspectives. A Nobel laureate much celebrated on both sides of the Atlantic, he preferred to keep himself off balance well into the ninth decade of his life by shuttling between Berkeley and Krakow, a beloved Polish city where he settled for good when his legendary robust health finally started to fail.

He has written about all this, with eloquence and force, in his essays, but also, indirectly, in his wonderfully condensed, intricate poems. Yet several years before his death in 2004 he offered a book that opens as an invitation to revisit, once again, the remembered landscapes of his life. "I went on a journey in order to acquaint myself with my province, in a two-horse wagon with a lot of fodder and a tin bucket rattling in the back," he writes in the opening passage of *Road-Side Dog*.[5] "It was so interesting to be moving, to give the horses their rein, and wait until, in the next valley, a village slowly appeared, or a park with the white spot of a manor in it. And always we were barked at by a dog, assiduous in its duty. That was the beginning of the century; this is its end."

Road-Side Dog is a strange book and in many ways a disappointing book — at least for those who expect from the author nothing but large historical vistas and intellectual distillation of the century. It is a book of fragments, snippets even, greatly diverse in form and in subject. It contains maxims, anecdotes, meditations, crumbs of worldly wisdom, introspections, shreds of theological and philosophical argument, poems. Some of these morsels are perfectly finished, self-contained miniature tracts, in the mode of the French *pensée*; others appear sketchy, tentative, even commonplace: assertions in search of proof, thoughts that should become essays, plotlines that need to be tested in a novel. Is this the writer's scrapbook offered generously — but also a little self-indulgently — to his readers, the literary equivalent of a rummage sale? But perhaps because of its loose, haphazard form, the book also sheds quite a bit of light on Milosz's lifetime fascinations, animosities, peeves, quarrels, visions, and misconceptions—everything, in short, that explains his greatness and some of his famous weaknesses. It is a small but important book—the closest thing we have to Milosz's literary testament.

Although Milosz declares himself an enemy of vain and pointless "literatures of confession," and his poetic self is usually that of an external, ironic observer, some of his most moving meditations in the book refer—discreetly, indirectly—to his personal experience of growing old. This happens also to be the theme of his book of poetry *Facing the River*, inspired by his first—since 1938—visit to his native Lithuania and published a few years before *Road-Side Dog*. In the long poem called "Capri" in *Facing the River* "a rejoicing and banqueting humanity" invites the speaker "to take part in the festivity of incessant renewal," but voices from his Lithuanian past demand a closing of accounts and call him back to the point of his departure, which may be also the point of conclusion. In *Road-Side Dog*, this tug between gravity and lightness is voiced in a lucid prose haiku: "Weakness of old age yet in my dreams wanderings in the mountains without effort, as in the poem by Po Chü-I, in which he, an old man, suddenly transformed in a dream, walks effortlessly with his stick." Later he adds, in an even more mystical tone, "Again I was flying in my dream. As if my old body contained, prior to live beings, the possibility of all movements, flying, swimming, crawling, running."

We are soon reminded, however, that what we are hearing is

not self-pity, but the reflection of a poet trying to sum up his past "taken as no more than a commentary to a couple of poems." In this stock taking, the physical and the sensual must not be omitted because they exist in a symbiotic, and sometimes embarrassing, relationship with the spiritual: "Poetry cannot be separated from awareness of our body. It soars above it, immaterial and at the same time captive, and is a reason for our uneasiness, for it pretends to belong to a separate zone, of spirit."

The double status of poetry, which seems to belong to the realm of the spiritual and to the realm of the material, is one of Milosz's recurrent motifs. He regards the act of writing poetry as a dubious occupation—a constant effort of the soul to overreach itself. The poet, and the artist more generally, is someone flawed, not completely adult, "not healthy, even if we confess it with difficulty." The luminosity of poetry, its "clear, solid, concise, nearly classical quality," has, in his view, a dark and dangerous source: it issues from "sorrow, grief, self-reproach, regret, shame, anxiety, desperation." This darker shadow of poetry, warns Milosz, should be treated with respect, never denied or hidden too deeply under the mask of overconfident form, lest the poet bring upon himself "the vengeance of the spinners of Fate."

Those who are familiar with Milosz's reverence for historical memory—his almost antiquarian love of old names and places, obscure facts, and cryptic historical references with which he fills many of his poems—will be surprised to read in a fragment called "Alexandria" that there may already be too much memory in the world. We live in an epoch, he remarks, "which is unable to forget anything." "Museums, libraries, photographs, reproductions, film archives. And amid that abundance individuals who do not realize that around them an omnipresent memory hovers and besieges, attacks their tiny consciousness." The author seems to caution that in an age when everything is mechanically recorded and instantly available, memory grows unstructured, haphazard, and eventually insignificant. Experience becomes an exercise in cross-referencing, a text engendered by endless other texts.

In another fragment of the book called "Archaeology," multitudes of past generations and cultures, swarms of departed souls, "move in unreal space, incessantly astonished by the rites, manners, and appearance of their successors, just as we would have been astonished if we'd been able to meet them." History, especially when it is considered in such extreme condensation, in a foreshortened millennial perspective, offends us with meaninglessness. This lack of scheme or direction, in turn, provokes a feverish, obsessive, often fallacious search for a meaning: "Something must correspond to something, something must result from something. Perhaps so that things just plain stupid and dishonest find an explanation."

Marxism, says Milosz, was just such an act of "inserting meaning" into history and more specifically into the history of the nineteenth century — an effort that spilled into the twentieth century with most unfortunate results. And "inserting meaning" into history is also the essence of utopian thinking, which is always more about the onerous present than about the radiant future. That is why Utopia is likely to remain a permanent feature of our imagined world. For Milosz, therefore, our present moment, marked as it is by a conspicuous lack of theories expounding the meaning or purpose of history, is exceptional and rather unsettling. Who knows what utopias wait around the corner?

The question of meaning—not only in history, but also in art, literature, and religion—is at the center of the question of modernity, which preoccupied Milosz from the beginning of his literary career. One of his most significant poems, "Treatise on Poetry," is a kind of versified history of the modern sensibility, from the decadence and dandyism of the turn of the twentieth century, through the spiritual and moral devastation of the two great European wars, to the embarrassing prostration of the twentieth-century thinking classes before the god of Historical Necessity. In *Road-Side Dog*, especially in the longer fragment called "Discreet Charm of Nihilism," Milosz writes similarly about two fundamental premises of modernity.

The first baleful premise is the "scientific paradigm," which has reduced the universe to "mathematical necessity." The second baleful premise is Nietzsche's proclamation that "there is no true world," which has undermined our trust in objective reality, including the reality of beauty and goodness. After such a pronouncement, Milosz suggests, the question what? has lost its meaning in both ethics and aesthetics and has been replaced by a ceaseless how? We have become "indifferent to content and react, not even to form, but to technique, to technical efficiency." Taken together, these claims created a world that Milosz considers hostile to spiritual aspirations. In one of the little fictional narratives in *Road-Side Dog*, even Darwin ponders the metaphysical consequences of the modern pattern of ideas and is forced to conclude that the "theology that can be drawn from it is nothing but that of the devil's chaplain."

The heart of the problem, Milosz seems to believe, is less the substance of such ideas than their democratization in our times: the phenomenon that may be called "trickle-down nihilism." "First, a fringe of the aristocracy cultivating literature and art, elegant, freed from the coarser superstitions. And churches filled with the pious, the scent of their incense and their prayers. They would come to a common frame of mind. It would take a hundred and fifty years." This, according to Milosz, is exactly the situation in which we find ourselves today. In the eighteenth and nineteenth centuries, it was an act of courage to pronounce the relativity of values and the illusory character of "objective" reality. Now it takes courage to dissent from those views.

Though clothed in beautiful metaphors and personal insights, this is a rather conventional line in the criticism of modernity and one that in our times appears less and less convincing. Outside of university seminars, radical nihilism is hardly the orthodoxy of the day. Churches in the Western world may no longer be full of the pious, but in America at least religious discourse and religious dogma make a triumphant return to public life and education, often in their most insidious, obscurantist form. If popular culture is any indication, we still prefer to see virtue rewarded and vice punished. Most members of modern societies, instead of wallowing in aristocratic decadence, work sixty hours a week, worry about their children's future, and live by the same unreflective, cautious, pragmatic moral code that has been typical of the toiling classes in all eras. The invention of the crisis of modernity—the radical division between then and now—appears to be yet another modern fallacy that confuses the history of ideas with history as such.

Luckily, Milosz is able to move beyond the household complaint about modern relativism. Premodern societies, he continues, derived their strength from the religious outlook that provided man with the sense of a special place and a special responsibility in the order of things. What troubles the Polish poet, however, is less the dissipation of the idea of God than the disappearance of the familiar images associated with religious systems. The premodern world was rooted not only, or not primarily, in theological doctrine, but in an iconography that organized the outer life and the inner life. If there was a "modern cataclysm," then, it happened mainly in the realm of imagination. "What has been lost," Milosz asserts, is the "vertical axis" that "rules everywhere in the non-corporeal" and "allows for a movement up to better incarnations, or down to inferior incarnations." Put differently, the spiritual destructiveness of the scientific worldview consists in undermining the old anthropocentric representation of the world and replacing it with inhuman, nihilistic imagery.

Yet Milosz observes that the new imagery could not completely win. Subconsciously, people have never relinquished their longing for the old images and notions. One of the consequences was a kind of vacillating imagination, which Milosz sees as largely responsible for the European Romantic movement, and which is the main subject of his most openly mystical book, *The Land of Ulro*. Taking as his main metaphor William Blake's mythical country of the dispossessed, the poet traces a sequence of desperate — often bizarre — efforts by some of the most imaginative modern minds to close the gap between the deep human need for mystery and the naturalistic flatness of the scientific worldview. He is fascinated by and feels affinity with everything that happens at the "frontier where religious and scientific imagination skirmished." In *The Land of Ulro*, for example, he describes how nondenominational mysticism drew liberally from the traditions of Christian Gnosticism, Jewish Cabala, and the occult, and how after the seeming defeats of organized religion a "second line of defense" was being formed by such visionary thinkers as Emanuel Swedenborg, Blake, and Johann Wolfgang von Goethe.

Milosz's own writing, especially his poetry, may be viewed as an attempt to counter this destruction by reclaiming the innocent ability to wonder and trust. One of the best examples is his early cycle of short poems "The World," written during the war, in which, by recreating the secure and radiant world of a child, he tries to restore a sacred kingdom in which "Faith is in you whenever you look / At a dewdrop or a floating leaf / And know that they are because they have to be," and "Hope is with you when you believe / The earth is not a dream but living flesh." In this sense, Milosz is right to call his work "essentially religious." "Instead of leaving to theologians their worries," he observes in *Road-Side Dog*,

> I have constantly meditated on religion. . . . In my lifetime
> Heaven and Hell disappeared, the belief in life after death was

considerably weakened, the borderline between man and animals, once so clear, ceased to be obvious under the impact of the theory of evolution, the notion of absolute truth lost its supreme position, history directed by Providence started to look like a field of battle between blind forces. After two thousand years in which a huge edifice of creeds and dogmas has been erected, from Origen and Saint Augustine to Thomas Aquinas and Cardinal Newman, when every work of the human mind and of human hands was created within a system of reference, the age of homelessness has dawned.

Again, a skeptic may object that in all likelihood a vast majority of people of all ages have lived in much more humble spiritual homes than those envisioned by Milosz. How, really, can we be sure about the real "contents of their imagination"? Besides, it takes a high degree of spiritual awareness to feel spiritually homeless in these times or any times.

Still, Milosz has no doubt about the need to reconstruct a more hospitable spiritual space for the human mind. This need has its root, he says, in our stubborn and seemingly illogical disagreement with the natural conditions of existence: suffering, death, injustice. "An atheist should accept the world as it is," he writes. "But then whence comes our protest, our scream: 'No!' Precisely this excludes us from Nature, determines our incomprehensible oddity, makes us a lonely species. Here, in a moral protest against the order of the world, in our asking ourselves where this scream of horror comes from, the defense of the peculiar place of man begins." And elsewhere in the book he remarks, "To recognize the world as ordinary is beyond strength. For me it is magnificent and horrible, impossible to bear. Everything indicates that either it was created by the devil or, as it is now, is the result of a primordial catastrophe. In the second case, the death on the cross of a divine Redeemer acquires full meaning."

In *Road-Side Dog*, Milosz wanders comfortably and freely among religious concepts and beliefs. He tries to breach the gap dividing consciousness and nature: "The mind would have been without grace had it not been anchored in matter: slaughterhouses, hospitals, cemeteries, pornographic films." He looks for systems in which the physical does not exhaust the possibility of Being, in which there is not nothing after death, in which human deeds are "imperishable" and good and evil have objective meaning.

Milosz is attracted to the austere abstraction of Buddhism. He dreams about a possible change within the scientific paradigm that would permit humankind to return to a more humane and humanist vision of the universe. He even quotes with curiosity a rather scary version of the intelligent design theory, in which the universe appears as a sort of game board, an experiment, or a simulation run by some superior beings. This view, as Milosz half-seriously remarks, would vindicate the polytheistic religions of antiquity, proving that the Greeks "had an intuitive grasp of the distance separating our will from a higher sort of calculation, indifferent to our desires and laments."

As if by an irresistible gravity of tradition, however, Milosz always returns to the Roman Catholicism of his upbringing. "I am grateful for that day," he writes, "when in a wooden little church between huge oaks I was admitted to the Roman Catholic Church. As well as for my long life, so that, believing or not believing, I could meditate on two thousand years of my history. That history was diabolic, no less than heavenly." His quarrel with Catholicism seems to be mostly political and temperamental. "I did not call myself a Catholic," he wrote in *Native Realm*, his autobiography, "because the word had such a definite political coloring in Poland. Besides, it would have been false if applied to me, considering my untamed, biological individualism. Nonetheless, I had brought from high school a knowledge of the abysses which, after all, would have to be fathomed sometime."[6]

But apart from that, Catholicism, with its two millennia of not always inspiring magisterium, with its rich cultural heritage and elaborate theological and philosophical dogma, remains for Milosz a valid framework for the exploration of his "doubts, turmoil, and despair." It also allows something like a second line of defense. For those who have been denied grace of faith, it offers Pascal's wager, or the agnostic's road to salvation: "What do we have to lose?"

Indeed, despite its medieval trappings and its seemingly immutable doctrines, the Roman Church has become a surprisingly welcoming sanctuary for modern agnostics and religious fellow travelers. In a fragment called "A Philosopher," Milosz presents an approving portrait of just such a person — an intellectual who describes himself as an atheist and who "would not seek in the existence of the universe any signs indicating its first cause." And yet he also cherishes religion as the fullest expression of "splendor and all the dignity of man" — especially religion, "in which the opposition between man and the natural order of things was the most marked, in which, therefore, man by liberating himself from that order achieved salvation." Convinced that civilization is in mortal danger, the philosopher decides to side, at least in his public statements, with the moral exhortations of the Vatican, or, in his own words, "to be counted among the workers in the Lord's vineyard." A nonbeliever, perhaps, but a godly nonbeliever.

On the one side, the "unfathomable depths"; on the other side, a moral ethos, a didactic program that can apparently function even without the element of faith: Milosz's Catholicism seems to be a versatile system. It is perhaps too versatile for those who wish to confront their belief, or their disbelief, unflinchingly, to meet the terms of the contract without looking for loopholes even when the consequences become uncomfortable. Milosz's meditations on religion also seek to show that life without some metaphysical dimension is practically unthinkable. He is unable, in other words, to imagine a true atheist — an individual who is convinced that the universe with God at its center is even more frightening, rife with contradictions, and absurd than a universe of "mathematical necessity." This sort of radical atheism always was a minority view, though it has a grandeur of its own as well as an ancient and noble pedigree. By not giving it a proper hearing, Milosz misses an important part of the puzzle — which is also his puzzle — of the millennia-long struggle of man with the concept of transcendence.

In some of his essays Milosz can sound like an angry prophet, impatient with his listeners' lazy materialism and their seeming disregard for the "great issues of humanity": the essence of reality, the nature of God, the meaning of history. His anger and passion sometimes make him restate those issues with almost dogmatic rigidity. But a closer look at his writing, especially his poetry, shows that searching for articles of faith — even his own, highly personal faith — is never really the main goal of his imaginative journeys. His last poems seem to alternate between fervent prayers to the Unknown and mischievous dissections of theological paradoxes and contradictions. In the last of his great poetic "treatises," "Treatise on Theology," he declares he does not wish to end his life as "a possessor of truth" and shrugs off "the serenity of faith" as "merely self-satisfaction." But he insists, not unlike another "atheistic Catholic," George Santayana, that humans' need to believe unverifiable truths seems to be rooted in their imaginative faculties. Nobody lives in the objective world, only in a world filtered through imagination, which can fashion the world into a home as well as a prison or a place of torment.

One of Milosz's poems in *Road-Side Dog* is a parable about a primitive tribe which, in between its slaughters and bloody rituals, polishes for generations a piece of granite into a huge, perfectly spherical ball:

> What did it mean to them? The opposite
> Of everything that passes and perishes?
> Of muscles, skin?
> Of leaves crackling in a fire? A lofty abstraction
> Stronger than anything because it is not alive?

The image of "leaves crackling in the fire" seems like a nostalgic, autumnal metaphor for the passage of time, but when it is read together with the preceding "muscles, skin," it calls forth much darker, more frightening associations. The somber closing phrase, "not alive," seems to negate the upward move-ment of "lofty abstraction," but it is also an invitation to explore its two possible meanings: dead or transcending the opposition of life and death.

Finally, the choice is ours, Milosz says, but we should be cognizant of the larger consequences of the choice: "Those fantasies, those pageants constructed by the human mind above the horror of life. All arts, all myths and philosophies: yet they are not limited to staying in their own lofty zone. For from them, from dreams of the mind, this planet arises, such as we know it, transformed and being transformed by mathematical equations." Are they just dreams? or maybe representations of something else, hidden behind the horizon of our senses? If Milosz knows the answer, he is keeping it to himself. All he is maintaining here, as throughout his whole literary work, is that the human self, the human mind, and the human soul cannot live solely in the empirical. Only what is born out of longings, dreams, and visions can constitute the self's true home.

This is the secret of the connection between poetry and reli-gion: they both create myths out of which reality arises. Even readers of a skeptical disposition can recognize the continu-ing, mad, inspired, inconclusive effort of the spirit described in these lines from "Capri":

> If I accomplished anything, it was when I, a pious boy, chased
> after disguise of the lost Reality.
> After the real presence of divinity in our flesh and blood which
> are at the same time bread and wine.
> Hearing the immense call of the Particular, despite the earthly
> law that sentences memory to extinction.

Shortly before his death in 1998, Zbigniew Herbert, one of the most original voices of postwar Central Europe, prepared his own, personal selection of eighty-nine poems from the nearly four hundred he had published.[1] The book closes with the poem "Pebble," which was originally published in 1961. A human hand comes in contact with a pebble, and both seem to recoil from the encounter, although, of course, we hear only the voice of the hand's owner. Like a timid suspect, he betrays his sense of guilt by his compulsion to talk, to explain, to rationalize. Like a seasoned interrogator, the pebble remains silent and looks at the man "with a calm and very clear eye."[2]

The man talks about the pebble's perfection — its sense of its limits, its unity, self-sufficiency, its stoic repose — but he really talks about himself, his volatility and the precariousness of life, his entrapment in his own subjectivity, his unresolved inner oppositions. By coming in contact with a part of the cold, inanimate universe the man realizes the strangeness of his own position in it: his thinking self appears as a disruptive, unwelcome cosmic presence. Man exists in the world, endlessly making and remaking himself, worrying about the meaning of his existence, looking for its structure and value. The pebble simply is — its being definitely not an issue to itself or anybody else. Hence the "heavy remorse" the narrator of the poem feels when the "false warmth" of his hand permeates the pebble's body.

The same remorse and envy of the pebble's scentless and still essence are present in the poetry of the American stone worshiper Robinson Jeffers, who thus addressed the ocean beating at "the boundaries of granite":

> It was long and long ago; we have grown proud since
> then and you have grown bitter; life retains
> Your mobile soft unquiet strength; and envies hardness,
> the insolent quietness of stone.

Every time I read Herbert's little existentialist parable, I have the impression that there is more in this poem than meets the eye — perhaps a key to a private riddle hidden in the seemingly open, well-lit edifice of his poetry. In the late 1980s, shortly before Herbert's final return to Poland in 1992, I visited him in his modest apartment in a less-than-elegant Parisian neighborhood. I smiled when, among piles of manuscripts, expensive art books, and photographs, I spotted a sizable pebble sitting on his desk.

Zbigniew Herbert died about a decade later, almost as he predicted in one of his last poems, amidst confusion and animosity caused by his harsh political statements, quarrels with long-standing friends, and clear signs of mental decline:

> my life
> should come full circle
> close like a well-built sonata
> but now I see clearly
> just before the coda

the broken chords
badly set colors and words
the din of dissonance
the tongues of chaos
("Breviary")

His health had been deteriorating for some time, and the last three volumes published during his lifetime, *Elegy for the Departure* (1990), *Rovigo* (1992), and *Epilogue to a Storm* (1998), have an unmistakably valedictory tone. When, in 1996, two years before his death, the Nobel Prize in Literature was awarded to Herbert's contemporary Wislawa Szymborska (only sixteen years after Czeslaw Milosz), for some in Poland the joy of this quite deserved distinction was mixed with a touch of sorrow, for they considered Herbert's achievements at least the equal of those of his two honored compatriots.

At the summits of poetry such contests are always a bit absurd. There is little doubt, however, that Herbert's impact on postwar Polish literature was unmatched by anybody else. At the time when Milosz was still a distant, albeit powerful star and Szymborska an occasional eruption of brilliance, Herbert almost singlehandedly introduced a whole new poetic idiom and changed the literary sensibility of Polish readers who matured in the turbulent sixties and seventies — between the student unrests of 1968 and the rise of Solidarity in 1980. It was for this younger group of readers, spared the experience of World War II and the worst excesses of Stalinism, that Herbert's writing became — to borrow the perfect phrase of the Polish dissident intellectual Adam Michnik — "a prayer of the generation."

But why Herbert, with his austere, seemingly monochromatic

diction, his classicist imagery and cadences, and his call to intellectual and moral rigor?

To begin with, his exemplary life made the dignity of his verse convincing and credible. The poet was born in 1924 in Lwow (now Lviv in Ukraine), which, together with Wilno (Vilnius in Lithuania), was to become one of the mythical Polish "lost cities" annexed by the Soviets during World War II. It is remarkable how many Polish writers, both contemporary and older, come from those multiethnic, contested, much-romanticized areas that for centuries composed the Great Duchy of Lithuania. Bruno Schulz is from Galician (now Ukrainian) Drohobycz. Milosz and the Polish novelist Tadeusz Konwicki were both born in Wilno, where the nineteenth-century Polish Romantic bard Adam Mickiewicz spent his formative years. Lwow is the birthplace of Stanislaw Lem, the author of philosophical allegories (disguised as science fiction fables), as well as of the poet Adam Zagajewski, who often evokes the city in his writing.

Zbigniew Herbert's father was a lawyer and a professor of economics — typical professions of well-settled, prudent Polish intelligentsia of the interwar period. (But family legend had it that his great-grandfather was an English gentleman related to the seventeenth-century metaphysical poet George Herbert.) World War II broke out when Zbigniew was fifteen. Like many young men of his generation, Herbert was involved in the anti-Nazi underground, although he rarely spoke about his experiences of that period. Only on one occasion, commenting on his apparent lack of leadership talents, he half-jokingly remarked that his gray hair actually dated back to the time when as a teenager he was "responsible for a handful of people."

Under the Nazi edict education above primary school was forbidden to Polish nationals. But Herbert earned his high school diploma by attending clandestine courses. He started writing during the war and published some of his poems in underground periodicals. One of his earliest poems, "Two Drops," tells about a pair of young lovers consumed by the fires of a collapsing world:

When it got very bad
they leaped into the other's eyes
and shut them firmly

So firmly they did not feel the flames
when they came up to the eyelashes
(M/S)

After the war Herbert followed his father's example and studied law and economics while pursuing his private interests in philosophy, theology, and history of art. He lived for awhile in Krakow, the ancient Polish capital miraculously spared the wartime destruction, then in Torun — the birthplace of Copernicus — and in Gdansk on the Baltic Sea, where the first shots of World War II were fired. In Gdansk, Herbert worked as a journalist reporting on postwar reconstruction and on archeological excavations revealing the intricate Polish-German-Scandinavian-Kashubian-Mennonite past of the old Hanseatic town. His articles, full of fascination with the tangled roots of civilizations, portend his later books of cultural essays, *Barbarian in the Garden, Still Life with a Bridle,* and *The Labyrinth on the Sea.*[3]

In the first years after the war there still existed in Poland residues of political and cultural pluralism. Herbert, though steering clear of the communist elites and their officially sponsored literary salons, was able to publish in Catholic periodicals that managed for awhile to maintain a degree of independence. When, around 1948, rigid Stalinist doctrine destroyed the last vestiges of political and cultural freedom and socialist realism became the only acceptable form of artistic expression, Herbert left the official Polish Writers' Union, thus sentencing himself to literary nonexistence. "I felt a powerful obligation to cut myself away from what was evil," he would explain later. The decision was not only difficult but seemingly irrevocable: "It required a reorientation of the whole life, a parting with hope, almost parting with one's youth." Between 1950 and 1955 he managed to publish some forty poems, but until the post-Stalinist political and cultural thaw of 1956 he had to support himself by means of clerical jobs in banks, cooperatives, and various associations.

Herbert's refusal to make even conditional ideological concessions to the communist regime was as absolute as it was simple. With characteristic self-deprecation, he would say later that although he needed to write, he did not need to publish — not that much, anyway. By contrast, Milosz, before his emigration to the West, served briefly (and without distinction) in the diplomatic service of communist Poland. Szymborska managed to produce two rather embarrassing books of socialist twaddle. Herbert was one of the very few Polish writers of that time who chose the Joycean stratagem of "silence, exile and cunning" rather than compromise. His delayed book debut, *Chord of*

Light, was published in 1956, when communist cultural policy eased enough to allow a degree of authenticity. Many Polish poets reached into their desk drawers to dig out their until-then-unpublishable works. Later, in a poem entitled "Drawer," Herbert recalled a certain sense of ambivalence about this sudden change from rebel into official cultural figure:

O drawer o lyre I have lost
and still so much that I could play
with fingers drumming your empty floor
and how good was a desperate heart
and how difficult to part
from nourishing pain which had no hope
(M/S)

One year later, in 1957, the poet was able to bring to light most of his secreted work. The result was his second book, *Hermes, Dog and Star*, which comprised no fewer than 101 poems. The two volumes marked not only the poet's second literary debut after a decade of silence, but also the second birth of Polish postwar poetry. The horrific experience of the war, Nazi occupation, and the Holocaust transformed the Polish poetic idiom. Gone were the post-Romantic sonorities and formalist conceits of the earlier generation. Polish poetry emerged from the war purified, linguistically minimalist, hard-bitten, and unsentimental. But its natural development had been arrested by the socialist realist cultural policy, with its forced optimism, requisite accessibility (poetry is for the masses!), and obligatory ideological avowals. Only after 1956 could Herbert's generation, including such poets as Tadeusz Rozewicz,

Szymborska, and the magician of Warsaw cockney (and therefore mostly untranslatable) Miron Bialoszewski, return to their natural poetic sensibility.

It was a time when writers' biographies were read as carefully, both by ordinary readers and by official censors, as their writing, and Herbert's biography was definitely part of his appeal to my generation, brought up in less dangerous but also more conformist and pallid times. Also attractive were his intellectual independence, his disdain for philosophical systems ("There are situations in which man should have the courage to live without a philosophy," he would write in his early, recently discovered sketch "Hamlet at the Boundary of Silence")[4] and his insistence on humans' absolute moral autonomy. For us, brought up in an aura of pervasive determinism—in its official Marxist-Leninist form and in the more pragmatic, geopolitical guise of much of the older Polish intelligentsia—Herbert's words carried a kind of almost pagan defiance: a conviction that although no man is the master of his fate, he is the absolute master of his acts. Many critics pointed out Herbert's close affinity with classical stoicism, with its absence of a personal God but an unwavering belief in natural law and the autonomy of the human soul. It was easy to notice that for Herbert the stoic virtue of *ataraxia* was never to be confused with "indifference." It was much closer to its original sense of "dauntlessness" or "intrepidity." It was a declaration of readiness to assert —quietly, without theatrical gestures—one's freedom and dignity under any conditions. Herbert used to remark that although he was raised a Roman Catholic, he was definitely more Roman than Catholic. For my profoundly skeptical generation

Herbert's proposition seemed like a long-sought response not only to Marxist determinism, but also to the ubiquitous, plaintive, romantic-nationalistic Catholicism of many of Marxism's opponents.

Herbert was the antithesis of Polish nationalism and parochialism. His constant cultural travels—his pilgrimages to Italy, Greece, France, and the Netherlands—evoked envy (he was one of the privileged few allowed to venture abroad) and painful longing for the unattainable aesthetic and sensual riches of the world. But they also created a sense of connectedness, ownership of that which was denied us by the near-impermeability of the famous curtain.

In an essay called "Holy Iona" Herbert writes, "It was then that I realized that I travel through Europe in order to extricate traces, signs of a lost kinship in the long, dramatic history of mankind. That is why a Romanesque column in Tyniec near Krakow, a tympanum from the church of St. Petronela near Vienna and a bas-relief in St. Trophim's cathedral in Arles were for me always not only a source of aesthetic experiences, but also a reminder that there exists a larger fatherland than the fatherland of my country."

This larger fatherland, for which we were especially grateful to Herbert, helped us to escape the often rigid cultural grip of the unhappy Polish tribe and to understand that we longed for something larger than just a better form of government or national sovereignty.

The generation Michnik refers to in his obituary note was clearly captivated by the poet's voice—reticent, poised, almost disembodied. It was a voice of courage shaped by millenniums of civilization and seemingly impervious to anxiety and doubt. In one of his most famous poems, "Envoy of Mr. Cogito," Herbert wrote,

> Go where the others went before to the dark boundary
> for the golden fleece of nothingness your last reward
>
> go upright among those who are down on their knees
> those with their backs turned those toppled in the dust
>
> you have survived not so that you might live
> you have little time you must give testimony
>
> be courageous when reason fails you be courageous
> in the final reckoning it is the only thing that counts

Such was, indeed, the prayer of our generation — disenchanted and ironic, but one that restored hope just as it seemed to be disappearing beyond the "dark boundary" of nihilism. Herbert's irony was perhaps one of the most attractive, and at the same time most confounding, aspects of his writing. It was definitely not the kind of irony that subverts and mocks all meaning. It was also not a brand of Romantic irony, which, according to Friedrich Schlegel, resulted from the clash between man's finiteness and his insatiable longing for the infinite. It was certainly not what D. J. Enright dismissed as impotent "wailing" at a world that fails to live up to our expectations.[5]

Some critics concluded that Herbert's irony, his habit of undercutting, usually in the very last lines of a poem, the very truth the poems seemed to be working toward, was nothing other than irony in the most classical, rhetorical sense: saying something shockingly fallacious in order to convince the listener that only the opposite could be true. But in Herbert the matter appeared a bit more complex. In his poetry, thesis and antithesis carry the same weight, although they seem to belong to two radically different domains: one ideal and the other narrowly real. This use of irony is best captured by Allan Rodway in his essay "Terms for Comedy" when he says that "irony is not only a matter of seeing a 'true' meaning beneath a 'false,' but of seeing a double exposure . . . on one plate."[6] The ironic statement becomes itself the object of irony. It subverts the ostensible message of the poem but in a way provokes the message to bite back. Evoking old myths of humanity will not save you from death. But is it really better to die in petrified silence? A hero in "Envoy" will be rewarded "with the lash of laughter with murder on a garbage heap" and "admitted to the company of cold skulls." But the skulls belong to the likes of Gilgamesh, Hector, Roland, so perhaps the company is not entirely undesirable. After taking a moral stand, you can expect that "your body's precious capital," the head, will roll to the ground ("The Power of Taste"). But in its fall the head will be transformed into a fragment of architecture — imposing even in ruins. The Golden Fleece will be reduced to "nothingness," but by the same token nothingness will gain the status of the Golden Fleece.

What is futile does not need to be meaningless. Righteousness may have no transcendental sanction, good and beauty may be merely ideas, but the thinking I, personified in Herbert's protagonist, Mr. Cogito, is real and spacious enough to sustain virtue in its confrontation with the world — to "enter into a covenant" with itself. And its struggle is hardly solitary: it is accompanied by echoes of the past, by the whole unending effort of humanity to define and protect its collective soul. Such is the world we have been given, declared the poet, yet within this world we are not without a moral choice, even if it is, as Mr. Cogito admits, "the choice of a gesture / the choice of a last word" ("Mr. Cogito on Upright Attitudes").

It was hard not to read Herbert's entreaties as direct allusions to immediate political facts familiar to Herbert's audience. In many instances such a reading was certainly justified. No one even perfunctorily familiar with postwar Polish history will miss the parabolic meaning of "Attempt at the Dissolution of Mythology": an underground anticommunist resistance unit, one of several that operated in Poland in the first years after the war, decides to give up its struggle and "enter rational society and somehow make do." A poem "To the Hungarians" (originally published without a title) pays homage to the fighters of the Hungarian uprising of 1956. "The Wall" captures the strange blend of despair and hope that characterized life under totalitarianism: A group of condemned prisoners stand against a wall waiting for the moment when "the fat bullet lodges itself in our necks." But there is also a tree behind the wall, and a star above: "The tree is lifting the wall with its roots. The star is nibbling the stone like a mouse. In a hundred, two hundred years there will be a little window."

Among the general public, especially in the seventies and eighties, Herbert was best known for his public poems, which touched upon current political events. When, in the late seventies, the opposition movement in Poland started to gain momentum, one of his most frequently quoted poems was "The

Power of Taste." The poet assumes the mask of a dandy for whom the intellectual poverty of an ideology is most evident in its aesthetics:

Before we assent we must examine closely
architectural forms rhythms of drum and fife
official colors homely rituals of burial

Our eyes and ears refused to submit
our princely senses chose proud exile

Many similar poems were printed in samizdat editions and recited at secret opposition meetings. Herbert's book *Report from a Besieged City* (1983), the first to be published by the Polish émigré house Kultura in Paris, was read as a chronicle of the state of war declared in Poland in 1981. Its verses certainly do not shun the pathos usually associated with nineteenth-century Polish Romantic poetry, like the title poem, which contains these well-known lines:

and if the City falls and one man survives
he will carry the City inside him on the paths of exile
he will be the City

These allusive, Aesopian elements in Herbert's poetry became the focus of many critics both in Poland and abroad. As political and intellectual dissent in Eastern Europe grew more outspoken and bold, it became habitual, almost reflexive, to interpret practically all cultural activity in this region as a covert expression of political views. The British critic Al Alvarez, who introduced East European literature to English readers in the sixties and seventies, wrote that it "takes on the patriotic, educative, and moral burdens normally assumed by the state." Poetry as a "witness to history" was a constant motif of Milosz's essays as well as of many of his poems. In many cases, this view of literature as mentor and consoler was certainly true. But in time it inevitably led to a one-sided, reductive reading of some of Poland's most complex writers.

Unfortunately, that was Herbert's fate. His American publishers consistently describe him as "a spiritual leader of the anti-Communist movement in Poland," a description most true poets would be loath to claim. Even those who valued Herbert's intricate irony and detected complexity under his seemingly transparent, declarative statements, worshiped Herbert primarily as a hope-giving voice of brightness and certitude — of stoic resilience, rationalist clarity, and moral authority made more palatable by his biting wit. "We feel that Herbert's poetry is eminently sane," wrote Milosz and Peter Dale Scott in the introduction to Herbert's *Selected Poems*, setting the tone for the poet's reception in the West.[7] "Control, conscience, honesty, and soberness are not always to be condemned, least of all when these are qualities of a poet who received a proper European initiation into horror and chaos."

Those interpretations, however, could be sustained only by scrupulously ignoring everything that did not fit Herbert's Apollonian image — his flashes of darkness, his unsettling dichotomies, his encounters with the uncertainty and pain that colored his poetry more frequently than his hagiographers and critics generally admitted. Herbert's last three books of poetry, *Elegy for the Departure*, *Rovigo*, and *Epilogue to a Storm*, and a

collection of his short, scattered prose published in English as
The King of the Ants revealed a more ambivalent, more somber
Herbert and prompted a careful rereading of the poet's earlier
works.[8]

The King of the Ants tells about the inexorable absurdity of
human history and of human fate. The volume is bracketed by
two stories that explore these two themes most directly. In the
first one, called "Securitas," Herbert invents a new Roman deity who symbolizes the caring, paternalistic idea of the state and
quickly becomes the patron of secret police, spies, and informers. The final piece retells the myth of the king of the Myrmidons, creatures that were half-human and half-ant, created
by the gods to alleviate the loneliness of their ruler. (The author
calls him Ajax, although he certainly means Aiakos, the grand-
father of Achilles and the Greater Ajax). Annoyed by the fact
that his subjects seem to be perfectly content with their simple,
antlike existence, the king undertakes a series of imaginative
and cruel experiments in order to induce among them social
discord, ambition, and anxiety—in other words, to launch
them into history. The attempt ends in complete disaster: "Ajax
knew that happiness implies movement, striving, climbing upward. But he did not know that progress, to use this ominous
word, was only an image, neither better nor worse than other
figments of the imagination." Both stories are obvious allusions
to Herbert's native realm. One of "the philosophers" employed
by Ajax to engineer the Myrmidons' history is called Jotvues,
which in Polish reads like J. V. S., or Joseph Vissarionovitch
Stalin.

Other stories in *The King of the Ants* focus less on history than on the absurd, incomprehensible fates of individuals. The story of Priam's wife, Hecuba, known from Euripides' "The Trojan Women," is told here in an almost Beckettian foreshortening. She is thrown into a dungeon; she tries to nurse a dead child; she turns into a she-wolf and leaps into the sea. Atlas, whose entire existence is reduced to the simple task of supporting heaven and who appears to Herbert as "the catatonic of mythology," becomes a hero of limitless, if involuntary, endurance, the "patron of those who are terminally ill, patron of those condemned to life in prison, those who are hungry from birth to death, the humiliated, all those who are deprived of rights, whose only virtue is mute, helpless, and immovable — up to a point — anger." The legendary athlete Cleomedes resembles heroes of Albert Camus' existential tragedies. He accidentally kills a man during a boxing match. Later, in a bout of madness, he slaughters a group of children and spends the rest of his life running from his people and his act. At the end, he dies in the slums of Corinth upon hearing that in his native land he is now worshiped as a god.

Myths are created in order to clarify the origins of things, the Polish poet tells us, and to insert meaning into the chaos of existence. But they may also be read as palimpsests with hidden meanings that have been rejected, concealed, as too dark or too disturbing to view in full light.

Is it possible to read Herbert in the same way? Darkness was certainly pouring into his poetry, and possibly into his life, around the time when most of the poems from his last three volumes were composed, but it was present from the beginning, especially in his early poems, in which he tries to bid farewell to the ghosts of his friends fallen during the war. One such poem, "Three Poems by Heart," originally appeared in *Chord of Light*. The first of its three movements is a search for a person, or rather for a language that could extract the memory of this person from among horrifying wartime images:

> I cannot find the title
> for a memory of you
> with a hand torn from the dark
> I move on the remains of faces
>
> faint profiles of friends
> froze into hard outlines

The second part of the poem speaks of the self-reproach of survivors who know that "our hands won't pass on the shape of your hands / we let them go to waste touching common things." The third movement introduces a disturbing contrast between images of life before the conflagration ("the children in our street / — such a torment to cats / the pigeons — a mild grey / in the park there was a statue of the Poet") and the horror that followed ("the children from our street / met with a very hard death / pigeons fell lightly / like air shot down").

In the last lines the destroyed city "flies to a lofty star / where the fire smells far / like a page from the Iliad." The starkly dispassionate language and the apparent stoic resolution of the poem (yes, it all has happened before) have a deeply unsettling effect. How can one reconcile heroic hexameters with the "very hard death" of a child?

Despite the horrifying connotations, these early poems still strive for a balance, a state that reconciles "motion with still-ness a line with a cry / trembling uncertainty simple clarity" ("Architecture"). But the poem "Oaks" from *Elegy for the Departure* sets a quite different tone. It starts like a romantic paean to the perfection of nature but soon changes into a vehement attack on nature's apparent disregard of suffering: "this Nietzschean spirit on a hushed sand dune / capable of soothing Keats's nightingale woes." Nature seems to be ruled by "a watery-eyed god with an accountant's face / a demiurge of contemptible statistics / playing with dice always fixed in his favor." Herbert's voice is growing more personal, his irony more astringent. His stoicism seems to break down in the face of very human and very elemental fear, as in "Prayer of Old Men," which ends on a mournful, pleading note:

> but do not allow
> the insatiable darkness of your altars
> to consume us
> tell us one thing
> that we will return

Even the most public poem in *Elegy*, "Mass for the Imprisoned," which, like "Report from the Besieged City," was inspired by the imposition of martial law in Poland in 1981, has an unusual melancholy, resigned tone. It is constructed almost exclusively of images of degraded landscapes ("clay pit," "burned sawmill," "flaking walls") and of human helplessness ("idle hands," "helpless elbows and knees," "mouths open as they sleep," a priest struggling to "tie and untie the knot").

There is little trace of the imperious contempt of the poem "The Power of Taste" or of the granite invulnerability of "The Envoy of Mr. Cogito." At the end of "Mass" the narrator assures us that the resistance will continue, but this time its only expression will be "worthy silence / and an intransigent barking of keys."

We seem to be very far from the realm of rational clarity and classical calm. But Herbert visited the darker regions of chaos and despair much earlier than in his last, somber volumes, and he even considered those visits a necessary condition of spiritual fullness. In "Hamlet at the Boundary of Silence" he writes, "Were it not for the tragic events that forced the prince out of his cocoon of study and contemplation, he would likely have remained until the end of his days in part a Stoic, in part an Epicurean, in part an Aristotelian. The sudden death of his father did not lend itself to rational interpretations." And he continues by making an unexpected declaration: "There are existential situations in which one has to forsake the system of gentle persuasions and convincing conciliations. Hamlet's greatness as a thinking being consists also in his passion for destruction, his nihilistic zeal, in the ardor of negation, in his burning skepticism."[9]

"In part a Stoic, in part an Epicurean, in part an Aristotelian" is how one of Herbert's early friends and tutors, the eclectic Polish philosopher Henryk Elzenberg (1887–1967), was often described by his colleagues. Herbert conducted a long, intense correspondence with Elzenberg in the 1950s and 1960s, and he owes him much of his doctrine of moral imperative that does not require any transcendental sanction but is rooted in culture and tradition — the real source and depository of ultimate human values. Herbert paid his master a moving tribute in the poem "To Henryk Elzenberg on the Centennial of His Birth," included in *Rovigo:*

> Your severe gentleness delicate strength
> Taught me to weather the world like a thinking stone
> Patient indifferent and tender all at once

But on more than one occasion Herbert signaled a lingering disagreement with his master's ideal of inner repose and stoic detachment. His poem "To Marcus Aurelius," dedicated to Elzenberg and published in *The Cord of Light*, is a lyrical treaty on the insufficiency of stoicism. The poem opens with a quiet, mournful "Good night Marcus," a clear echo of "Good night, sweet Prince," but soon rises in a dramatic crescendo when the philosopher-king's study (and the stately, classical rhythm of the poem) is disrupted: "this the barbarian cry of fear, / your Latin cannot understand" (M/S). The poem ends with the "defenseless tears" of the disciple, who implores his master to "hang up your peace / give me your hand across the dark."

In his writings and lectures Elzenberg used to point out that the human mind is a part of the Cosmos and therefore it is wrong, even for an atheist, to perceive the Cosmos in purely materialistic terms. Reality is suffused with ideas and meanings generated by the mind. By creating meaning man creates his own universe, his own "world against the world." Similar concepts are present in several of Herbert's poems, but so is profound doubt in the spiritual self-sufficiency of humankind:

we with the astronauts' white cane
awkwardly we bump into stars
we see nothing we hear nothing
we beat with our fists on the dark ether
on all the wavelengths is a whining

Even when the human mind seems to triumph over despair, Herbert is keenly aware of the narrow, perilous path we must navigate between the world of ideas and the ever-present, often horrifying raw matter of life. In "Path" he describes a journey through "the forest full of berries and flitting spirits" along a path that "all of a sudden / lost its unity" and confuses our sense of direction. On the right side of the path, hidden in deep shadows, lies "a source," "the moist heart of things," "the dark kernel of the cause." On the left side is "a hill" of reason, which offers "peace and a general view," a "soothing knowledge the forest is one of many." But each of these two, seemingly incompatible vistas leaves out an essential part of experience. Thus the poem ends in complaint: "Is it truly not possible to have them together / the source and the hill the idea and the leaves."

Behind Herbert's calm, measured sentences, behind his stoic composure and moral resolve, behind his clarity and reason — humans appear as infinitely vulnerable and confused beings constantly assaulted by history and nature, uncertain of their place in the universe, tormented by primal pain and fear. No wonder that these brittle reeds envy the permanence of stones, the splendid self-sufficiency of inanimate objects. In "White Stone," which reads like an earlier version of "Pebble" (it was published in *Hermes, Dog and Star*), the narrator states,

deeper than earth's blood
more luscious than a tree
there is the white stone
an indifferent plentitude

Similarly, in "Wooden Die," "Objects," " Stool," and "Careful with the Table" objects either silently disparage man or try to offer questionable consolation by flaunting their perfect immutability and lack of "inner life." In the essay "Among the Dorians" in *Barbarian in the Garden* Herbert recounts a Promethean legend according to which men and stones, although representing two different cosmic orders, were actually blood relatives. And it was probably stones that chose the better part — hardness rather than fleshy softness, solid endurance instead of fragile existence. In his early poems "A Testament" and "Trembles and Heaves" we sense something like a Buddhist longing for nonbeing, because the incredible variety of life hides innumerable forms of suffering and decay. Winter in "Winter Garden" deserves praise because under its cover "amid the lowest plants unrest froze like a lizard." This only partly ironic, one can presume, praise of deadly immobility returns in another poem of the same title in *Inscription* (1969), where winter vanquishes "the earth of sticky paws / digging in the remains of flowers" and reconstructs the garden as a pure abstraction, "from rhomboids triangles pyramids."

In his real and imaginary travels through the world of art, Herbert shows a particular affinity to geometry, balance, and hard, rough surfaces. In Orvieto he discovers "it is possible to render in stone the creation of light" and hears how "the slow breathing of stones rises and sinks under the plaster." In Luca Signorelli's "The Coming of the Antichrist" he admires three angels "like balanced triangles with wings." Among all the arts he favors the most objective ones — painting, sculpture, and architecture — and reserves his highest praise for the perfect blending of all three. In a fragment of Duccio's "Maestà," he says, "leaves are like small sapphires; the hide of the donkey in flight from Egypt is like gray granite; and the snow on the bare, truncated cliffs glitters like mother of pearl." He admires Romanesque architecture's trust of "geometry, simple numerical rule, the wisdom of the square, balance and weight." The essay about northern Gothic, "A Stone from the Cathedral," is a prose poem about those who labor in stone: architects, masons, bricklayers, quarry workers — with their secret rituals and geometric signs that survive in Freemasonry. He adores Piero della Francesca as a master of geometry who absorbs passion and creates "eternal order of light and balance" even while depicting the most cruel and tumultuous scenes. About Piero's "The Flagellation of Christ" he says, "The compositional threads are cool, taut and balanced. Each person stands in an exact construction like a rock of ice, which at first glance seems under the rule of the demon of perspective."

This insistence on symmetry, geometry, and rigid form was often quoted as proof of Herbert's love of classical order. But the opposition between humans and objects, between life and geometry, between fibers of reality and abstractions constantly recalled in his writing suggests a disturbing ambiguity at the heart of human culture. A lot has been written about the poet's pilgrimages to the masterpieces of Greece, Italy, France, and the Netherlands recorded in his essays. The descriptions of his encounters with masterpieces, with cities, and with landscapes shaped by the human hand impart true aesthetic joy. But for Herbert, Art and Beauty do not promise anything better than this world. Unlike his younger colleague Adam Zagajewski, Herbert does not see masterpieces as flickers of divine, transcendental light miraculously penetrating our own dark realm. For Herbert, they are desperate, ultimately futile attempts to delay the inevitable decay of everything beheld by our senses and our mind. Hence the unmistakable tone of nostalgia and regret that accompanies his visual enchantments.

Herbert also scorns aesthetes who treat high culture as a precious ornament on the edifice of civilization. For him, culture is the very skeleton of humanity — its form and substance — but also a product of painful friction between raw, living flesh and the hard, indifferent surface of reality. It is humanity's self-image fashioned in order to exorcise our self-fear and self-loathing. Not accidentally, *Barbarian in the Garden* opens with a visit to prehistoric cave paintings in Lascaux, France, in which the author detects a sense of shame at the core of the just-awakened human self-consciousness. From the dawn of history, the poet seems to suggest, man was equally tempted and repulsed by the "source" of his innermost being, the "dark corn" of prehuman instincts. Out of this ambivalence was born the millennia-long climb up the "hill" of culture, where things appear solid and clear and where a "general view" allows us to look at ourselves from the outside, as entities to be examined in dispassionate curiosity.

For Herbert, culture not only imposes order upon the disorderly life, but also transforms subjectivity into objectivity, fluidity into substance, experience into a thing. It is a part of humanity's existential struggle with itself, a part of Elzenberg's "creation of the world against the world." That is why, in "Mr. Cogito and Pop," Herbert dismisses those cultural trends that try to return to humanity's primal source: "to drag from the guts / what's in the guts / terror and hunger." The poet dismisses the soul's primal scream because / "a cry eludes form / is poorer than a voice." The cry will always be there, and at times a cry seems the only true expression of pain, says the poet, but mere expression solves nothing and leaves us as exposed as we were before. The true function of culture is to go beyond the expression of man's hurt. Culture must help man "isolate it in yourself / and if it is possible / make from the stuff of suffering / a thing or a person" ("Mr. Cogito Reflects on Suffering").

Herbert seems to indicate that all cultural endeavors consist in turning existence into things, formlessness into form. This holds true for things material — paintings, sculptures, cities — and immaterial — myths, aesthetic canons, moral commandments, which also assume in his writing the weight and substance of palpable objects. That is why moral imperatives are treated as absolute despite their apparent lack of transcendental sanction. In "Priest" the celebrant offers sacrifices to emptiness, but there is something noble and necessary in those offerings made to "a deity / without a head" (M/S). We may dwell in existential void and construct our lives out of void, but through our actions the void can assume a shape and a meaning — like the abstract, mysterious, purely hypothetical entity that slowly materializes in the poem "Study of the Object." Ethics, aesthetics, epistemology, and ontology are intimately interconnected: by casting out the moral imperative, by stepping out of his self-created form, humankind becomes obscure and unbearable to itself and eventually dissolves into nothingness.

When *Barbarian in the Garden* appeared in English, Al Alvarez wrote in a review that its title implies that Herbert sees himself as "the barbarian outsider reacting to the civilized gardens of France, Italy and ancient Greece."[10] Herbert never suggested, however, that "being civilized" consists in growing up in the vicinity of world-class museums or architectural treasures. In fact, his loving descriptions of the fruits of artistic genius are interspersed with accounts of horrifying acts of barbarity — wars, immolations, torture, religious and political persecution — committed in their very shadow. Herbert's title seems to suggest that the garden has been planted by the barbarians — that beauty, art, symmetry are twin sisters of pain, fear, and inner chaos. When, in "Wawel," he describes himself as "a barbarian / who from crosses and gallows / learned how the mass is balanced," he speaks not only for his native East European realm. But he may suggest that his specific vantage point in an oppressed and broken country allows him to better understand the hidden connection between the dark "source" and the shining "hill."

Herbert also indicates that "high culture" must stay aware of its dark roots lest it become aloof and complacent, believing it is a separate, divine domain governed by its own set of rules. Herbert's poetry has been called Apollonian, although on many occasions he declared himself an acolyte of the trickster god Hermes. In fact, Apollo, the embodiment of perfect, autonomous, self-contained beauty, functions in Herbert's private mythology as a highly ambivalent figure. In "Apollo and Marsyas" the god commits a horrible sin of pride: he orders the flaying of a sylvan Marsyas for challenging him to a musical duel. We see him walking away, disgusted with Marsyas's cries of pain. He muses, very much like Mr. Cogito in his meditations on pop, on the aesthetic poverty of the raw, biological "truth" of his victim's torment. But just as his victory seems complete, a petrified nightingale falls to his feet. Marsyas's pain has produced a thing—perhaps one of the primitive animal figures offered to assuage the wrath of Greek gods.

Tension within culture endlessly fleeing and constantly returning to its paradoxical source is probably the most intriguing subject of Herbert's poetry—far more important than his political parables and allusions. It also reveals Herbert as a poet whose vision of humankind in the universe is almost unredeemably dark, although it does not preclude individual dignity and existential heroism. His man secretly envies stones, dreams about crawling back into inanimate, unfeeling matter.

In *The Elegy for the Departure, Rovigo,* and *Epilogue to a Storm* a tone of resignation, new in his poetry, appears. The poet confesses that the seemingly magical journey of his life "in fact / was a breakneck journey / tangled roads / apparent aimlessness / fugitive horizons," while his fate unfolded practically without his participation ("Clouds over Ferrara"). In those volumes time gets shorter, the universe shrinks, beauty ceases to shine, beloved objects inevitably slip from human grip.

A similar transformation takes place within the structure and language of the poems. Instead of Herbert's familiar verbal austerity, his dignified, rhythmical phrasing and descriptive precision, we encounter processions of surreal, cryptic images, discords, and nightmares. Granite, marble, wood — materials of stability and structure — give way to dirt, clay, straw, manure, sand, and limestone. Irony disappears almost entirely, and references to art, history, and mythology become ambiguous and rare. All this communicates a sense of man's nakedness, an acute and very personal awareness of human weakness and vulnerability. There is even an occasional note of anger at beauty that

> tries to ennoble
> to raise to a higher level
> praise in song dance and chatter
>
> decayed human matter
> washed-out suffering
> ("A Mirror Wanders the Road")

The central image of this period is Rovigo, one of very few Italian towns apparently lacking in historic or artistic distinction. It is not a mythical city but a real town, of "blood and stone," where "a man died yesterday someone went mad / someone coughed hopelessly all night." It is a waiting room, a place "Reduced to its station to a comma a crossed-out letter / nothing just a station — *arrivi – partenze.*"

It is Rovigo — Herbert seems to say — not radiant Orvieto, Siena, Arles, that is our real native city, the place to which we must pay homage before our final *partenza*. It is, after all, our true home, even if it is also a dark, frightening place. In "Prayer of Old Men," from *Elegy for the Departure of Pen, Ink and Lamp,* death appears as "a return to the lap of childhood / to a great tree to a dark room."

The title poem in *Elegy for the Departure* is a lament for the three objects presented here both as companions of studious childhood and symbols of the three ideas most often associated with the Herbertian, presumably classicist vision: the critical mind, a "gentle volcano" of imagination, and "a spirit stubbornly battling" the darker demons of the soul. We learn that the departure of the objects was caused by some unspecified "infidelity" on the part of the speaker, and that it leaves him feeling guilty and powerless. The last words of the poem, and of the book ("and that it would be / dark"), sound like a door slammed shut.

And yet, strangely, while reading Herbert's late poems, we also feel that the final line, that of despair, is never crossed. When everything else departs there remain, still, courage, strength, the moral imperative with hope and faith stubbornly clinging to its fibers. The echo of "The Envoy of Mr. Cogito" ("be courageous when reason fails you be courageous / in the final reckoning it is the only thing that counts") returns in *Rovigo* in a less grand, yet recognizable form in "Orwell's Album": "But he'll never surrender. / And he goes off like a pendulum patient and suffering / to a certain encounter." In "Journey," another valedictory poem in *Elegy*, Herbert takes us on a solemn tour of an individual life — from the first intellectual and sensual initiations, through "abandoned drifts of myths and religion" and endlessly expanding horizons, until the point at which the world begins to contract, "the clock stops," and the voyager must "yield the air to another." So how does it end, in victory or in defeat? or is that the right question? Certainly, it is not a question a pebble, a star, a broken piece of marble would condescend to ask, the author seems to say. The last lines of the poem offer the following summing-up of Herbert's paradoxical yet steadfast belief:

> So if there is a journey pray that it be long
> a true journey from which you do not return
> a copying of the world an elemental journey
> a dialogue with nature an unanswered question
> a pact after a battle
>
> a great atonement

Wislawa Szymborska, who received the Nobel Prize in Literature in 1996, must be one of the most reticent or most self-discerning poets of today. In a literary career spanning more than half a century, she is willing to acknowledge only some two hundred of her poems collected in several slender volumes. This sparse body of work, however, displays unusual diversity and polychromy. She defies all the usual terms (classicist, linguistic, moralist) used to classify Polish writers of her generation. She shares some characteristics with all these schools but clearly belongs to none. She practices isolation both in her writing and in her life, avoiding autobiography and remaining intensely private.

Born in 1923 in Kornik, near Poznan, Szymborska spent her childhood and early youth in wartime Poland. She started to publish poems in literary periodicals just after the war, in the brief period of relative political and cultural liberty terminated in 1948 by the overt Stalinization of much of communist-controlled Europe. When she tried to publish her first volume of verse, it was rejected for less than perfect adherence to the prescribed model of socialist realism style. Like many of her contemporaries, she was faced with the alternatives of silence or compromise.

Some of her peers, like Zbigniew Herbert and the experimental linguist poet Miron Bialoszewski, chose to remain silent and survive doing menial jobs until, in 1956, the political strictures were partly (and temporarily) relaxed and they could again start publishing their work. Others, out of conviction or cynicism, accepted the role of court poets of the new regime. Szymborska did compromise, at least in part, with the formal and thematic demands of socialist culture while at the same time struggling to maintain some degree of authenticity and traditional liberal-humanistic values (known as intelligentsia values in Poland) endangered by the spiritual desolation of the Stalinist years.

The painful attempts to stay within the officially sanctioned current of Polish culture and yet to avoid the ultimate lie are reflected in her first two books of poetry, *That's What We Live For* (1952) and *Questions Put to Myself* (1954). The first volume, later wholly repudiated by the poet, contained the usual variations on officially prescribed optimistic themes of the new, better life rising from the ruins; however, their gentler, more lyrical tone sharply distinguished them from the standard poetic production of that kind. The second book showed a retreat into more private, contemplative themes of love, death, and memory that were occasionally tolerated under the cultural policy of that period. Only after the political thaw in 1956, and with the publication of her third volume, *Calling Out to Yeti* (1957), was Szymborska to find her true poetic voice.

Poetry has remained her only occupation. She has published little prose except for short, witty book reviews which appeared regularly in a Polish literary magazine—most of them on ostentatiously nonpoetic subjects: popular science, entertainment, dictionaries and encyclopedias. Only rarely did she lend her voice to public issues. In the late 1970s she showed her solidarity with her dissident colleagues by placing her signature on protest letters and by supporting underground cultural ventures. Yet in her writing she remained in a sense one of the most apolitical of Polish writers during the intensely political two decades leading up to the Solidarity rising. She accepted the Nobel in literature gracefully and modestly but scrupulously avoided the usual celebrity circus, gratefully entrusting her friend and colleague Czeslaw Milosz with the public role of the "official" Polish Nobelist.

Szymborska is often compared with two of her contemporaries, the ironic classicist Zbigniew Herbert and the disenchanted existentialist Tadeusz Rozewicz, both of whom belong to the same generation and share with her the main experiences of the epoch. Indeed, some of her poems display the Herbertian search for classical balance and symmetry as a protection against the pressure of the chaotic, unsettled modern world, as well as Herbert's love of cultural allusion and parabolic message. On other occasions she appears to opt for the stark, direct style reminiscent of Rozewicz. But if the poetry of Herbert and Rozewicz seems essentially monochromatic and constructed of solid verbal masonry, hers is a much more supple, multicolored, one could say organic medium. In Herbert's work we encounter the skeptical Cartesian Mr. Cogito; Rozewicz's voice is almost invariably that of a hardened, sardonic survivor. Szymborska presents us with a less defined but much more emotive persona who often speaks in the voice of a woman, a child, even a small animal. As a rule, those speakers refuse to view the human drama "from above," as detached observers and commentators. They wonder, hesitate, try to meet life on its own terms, and, like the scoffing space travelers in "Warning," they are "happiest in the cracks / between theory and practice, / cause and effect."[1]

The language and the poetic perspective in Szymborska's writing convey the sense of deliberately chosen vulnerability and a quizzical openness to life's contingency:

> Why after all this one and not the rest?
> Why this specific self, not in a nest,
> but a house? Sewn up not in scales, but skin?
> Not topped off by a leaf, but by a face?
> Why on earth now, on Tuesday of all days,
> and why on earth, pinned down by this star's pin?
> ("Astonishment")

Szymborska can be highly sophisticated, pursuing involved philosophical questions in what she calls essay poems, but sometimes she imperceptibly shifts into a seemingly playful, tongue-in-cheek light verse mode. In fact, some of her poems have been used as lyrics of popular songs. She writes with equal relish about a bodybuilders' contest ("From scalp to sole, all muscles in slow motion. / The ocean of his torso drips with lotion") and on Heidegger's concept of Nothingness. She can be playfully commonplace and strikingly eccentric. She struggles for the utmost precision of expression, yet engages in complicated linguistic games. Most important, she is a poet of modern experience often hiding behind the mask of an innocent still capable of asking naive questions about the meaning of life and the origins and nature of evil.

Szymborska belongs to the generation of Polish writers who, in young adulthood, witnessed some of the worst atrocities of the century, events which left a lasting impression on their terse, restrained language and their dark, disenchanted world-view. It is not surprising, therefore, that a subtle, intelligent, often ironic meditation on mortality seems to be the unifying theme of much of her poetry. Her more recent poems include a number of moving valedictions addressed to deceased friends. Yet the theme of perpetual, universal fading and departing — not only of people, nations, and living organisms but also of memories, images, shadows, and reflections — was present in her poetry from the very beginning. The poem opening the best-known selection of her poems in English translation, Stanislaw Baranczak and Clare Cavanagh's *Poems New and Collected 1957–1997*, and written when the poet was in her thirties, contains a moving invocation to an ideal death:

> When it comes you'll be dreaming
> that you don't need to breathe;
> that breathless silence is
> the music of the dark
> and it's part of the rhythm
> to vanish like a spark.
> ("I'm Working on the World")

One of the recurrent motifs in Szymborska's poetry is a kind of existential contest between living, that is, mortal, beings and inanimate matter, which often serves as a reminder of life's impermanence and imperfection. The theme closely resembles the preoccupation with objects as humans' competitors and judges found in Herbert's poetry. In Szymborska's "Museum," life is presented as a race—decided, we are made to believe, long before it started—between the human body and objects, in which "The crown has outlasted the head. / The hand has lost out to the glove. / The right shoe has defeated the foot." Free of the inner division into mind and matter, almost impervious to time and unable to experience pain, objects evoke the admiration and envy of perplexed human beings. In "Conversation With a Stone," which reads almost like a variation on Herbert's "Pebble," the poet knocks "at the stone's front door," demanding to be allowed to partake, at least for a moment, of its tranquil, if inhuman, reality. Unlike the pebble in Herbert, however, Szymborska's stone breaks its stoic silence to mock the human supplicant: " 'You shall not enter,' says the stone. / 'You lack the sense of taking part.' "

Whereas in Herbert's verse life strives to imitate stone, groping for hard, unbendable support—in "ancient incantations of humanity" or moral canons—in Szymborska living creatures are usually reconciled with their natural fragility. If inanimate objects represent the ultimate economy of existence, living organisms epitomize its magnificent, if also extravagant and wasteful, generosity. In "Returning Birds," birds have migrated too early from their winter grounds ("Rejoice, O reason: instinct can err, too") and now are dying of cold:

a death
that doesn't suit their well-wrought throats and splendid claws,
their honest cartilage and conscientious webbing,
the heart's sensible sluice, the entrails' maze,
the nave of ribs, the vertebrae in stunning enfilades,
feathers deserving their own wing in any crafts museum,
the Benedictine patience of the beak.

The last word in the poem belongs, again, to a stone that comments "in its own archaic, simpleminded way" on life as "a chain of failed attempts."

It is possible to read such a passage as a general meditation on life's frailty that seems to mock and contradict its amazing complexity and beauty. Those familiar with the poet's native realm, however, will guess that it is probably the memory of war and the Holocaust that engenders her imagery and gives it an unmistakably moral resonance. Her most famous poem about the Holocaust, "Still," uses an elaborate formal device in which the horror is told in gentle, almost lullaby-like cadences that in the last stanza break into a hysterical crescendo. There are moments, however, when despite the author's taciturn tone and proclivity to ironic form the experience of her wartime generation speaks through her poems directly and with shattering force. "Write it down. Write it. With ordinary ink / on ordinary paper: they weren't given food, / they all died of hunger." Thus begins the poem "Starvation Camp Near Jaslo." The Nazi death camp in Jaslo, in southern Poland, was one of those places where inmates were crowded into an empty, fenced space and left to die a slow death of hunger and exposure. This is not an easy subject for a poem, but Szymborska handles it master-fully by reversing the pastoral image of nurturing nature:

> Sunny. Green. A forest close at hand,
> with wood to chew on, drops beneath the bark to drink —
> a view served round the clock,
> until you go blind. Above, a bird
> whose shadow flicked its nourishing wings
> across their lips. Jaws dropped,
> teeth clattered.

This is less a moral indictment than an expression of existential horror that an event like this could somehow become a part of the human experience. The horror is deepened by the ano-nymity of death — the erasure of memory that inevitably fol-lows an act of genocide. In the same poem, Szymborska writes,

> History rounds off skeletons to zero.
> A thousand and one is still only a thousand.
> That one seems never to have existed:
> a fictitious fetus, an empty cradle,
> a primer opened for no one,
> air that laughs, cries, and grows,
> stairs for a void bounding out to the garden,
> no one's spot in the ranks.

One of Szymborska's poems, as well as a book published in 1976, is entitled "A Large Number," and the notion of statisti-cal abstraction often figures in her poems as a kind of death's double, a shadow that enters the stage after the massacre to wipe out the stains and to prepare the ground for new atroci-ties. It is, therefore, a moral duty to remember everything that is singular—to save and preserve the concrete, particular facts, moments, and sensations, to replace "great numbers" with "individual faces" and "unique eyes." For Szymborska the joy of writing consists in "The power of preserving. / Revenge of a mortal hand."

And yet this labor of memory is also increasingly difficult and frustrating. The past and the present have become too crowded and chaotic, the well of time too deep and murky. When, in the poem "Census," no fewer than seven cities are uncovered at the site of mythical Troy, "Hexameters burst" while multitudes unrecorded in verse clamor in vain for our attention:

> We three billion judges
> have problems of our own,
> our own inarticulate rabble,
> railroad stations, bleachers, protests and processions,
> vast numbers of remote streets, floors, and walls.
> We pass each other once for all time in department stores
> shopping for a new pitcher.
> Homer is working in the census bureau.
> No one knows what he does in his spare time.

Cities without their own epic, the author suggests, can easily share the fate of Atlantis, "Hypothetical. Dubious. / Uncommemorated. / Never extracted from air, / fire, water, or earth" ("Atlantis"), or even that of Hiroshima from the poem "Written in a Hotel," which, unlike the more celebrated Kyoto, was considered one of countless "inferior cities" of the world, undistinguished enough to be "safely" erased from the face of the planet.

Many of Szymborska's poems are laments on the insufficiency of human perception that leaves so much of the world

unnoticed, undescribed, "beyond the reach / of our presence."
In "A Large Number," she speaks of this anguish directly:

> My choices are rejections, since there is no other way,
> but what I reject is more numerous,
> denser, more demanding than before.
> A little poem, a sigh, at the cost of indescribable losses.

The thought that the human mind may be the only mirror in
which the universe can see its own reflection—perhaps its only
recourse to nonbeing—is in Szymborska's poetry a source of
constant guilt, guilt which sometimes reaches an almost religious intensity:

> My apologies to everything that I can't be everywhere at once.
> My apologies to everyone that I can't be each woman and each
> man.
> I know I won't be justified as long as I live,
> since I myself stand in my own way.
> ("Under One Small Star")

At the heart of Szymborska's poetry lies a preoccupation with
the human mind—the mystery of its origin and purpose, its
ability to create and annihilate whole internal universes, its
strange existence within both the natural and the ideal world,
its seemingly infinite capacity and striking shortcomings, and,
finally, the inexplicable disquiet it feels whenever it turns its
lens upon itself. In "A Note" a visitor to an anthropological
exhibit looks at primitive stone tools and ponders the resemblance between "the spark struck from stone / and a star" and
decides that this resemblance "lured us out of the depths of our
kind," giving birth to humanity:

Out of the stone
the sky flew.
A stick branched out
into a thicket of ends.
A snake raised the sting
from the tangle of its reasons.
Time staggered
in the rings of trees.
Multiplied in the echo
was the wailing of the awakened.
(JT)[2]

The origins of humanity, or rather humanness, are also the subject of "The Cave," which takes us into the now empty and silent womb where human passion, fear, desire, cruelty, and ecstasy were born. The poem ends with the question whether the whole journey was an accident or some kind of necessity:

On earth, maybe the only one
in heavens? seventh heaven?
        You headed out of emptiness
and you truly want to know.
(JT)

What was born in the cave, Szymborska seems to suggest, was also metaphysical doubt, which she sees less as a philosophical or religious problem than a permanent resonance of all human thought. In a mysterious poem "Pursuit," the modern, skeptical self chases after elusive entities, sometimes resembling ancient gods, which always manage to "vanish in time":

All I can do is stoop and pick up a pebble
which isn't going to tell me where they went.

They don't like leaving me any clues.
In the art of erasing evidence, they are unrivaled.
(JT)

When the narrator finally steps on some leaping, wiggling creature, he discovers that "it is but a shadow, too much my own to feel I've reached my goal."

The "wailing of the awakened"; the native cave filled with emptiness; man chasing after God but stepping on his own shadow: Szymborska's vision is unmistakably existentialist and dark. In her universe, humankind is alone, unaided by any transcendental guidance, his perceptive faculties and moral instincts evidently not up to the task with which they have been burdened. Unable to hold in his mind the plurality and diversity of being, he seems doomed to reduce it first to abstractions and then to ashes. Still, it would be hard to classify this vision as entirely pessimistic. The poet's reluctance to become yet another prophet of doom is evident in "Soliloquy for Cassandra," in which the eponymous doomsayer ponders the futility of her prophetic powers. She loved the people of Troy but loved them "From heights beyond life. / From the future. Where it's always empty / and nothing is easier than seeing death." Those who did not want to hear the prophecy are dead,

> But in them they bore a moist hope,
> a flame fuelled by its own flickering.
> They really knew what a moment means,
> oh any moment, any one at all
> before —
> It turns out I was right.

Thus Szymborska is determined not to discount the "moist hope" completely. In "Reality Demands," she takes us on a tour of the famous slaughter grounds of history—from Actium and Chaeronea, through Kosovo Polje and Borodino, to Verdun and Hiroshima—to show that they in fact are places like any other, with gas stations, ice cream parlors, holiday resorts, and busy factories. "So much is always going on, / that it must be going on all over," she says. "Perhaps all fields are battlefields, / those we remember / and those that are forgotten." Should we be horrified or relieved by that realization? "What moral flows from this?" asks the poet. "Probably none. / Only the blood flows, drying quickly, / and, as always, a few rivers, a few clouds." The universe does not want to yield a direct answer, but it does not preclude a search for one, either:

> I prefer keeping in mind even the possibility
> that existence has its own reason for being.
> ("Possibilities")

This may not be much of a consolation—says the Polish poet's quiet, intelligent voice—but it is the only one we have and perhaps the only one we need.

GUSTAW HERLING-GRUDZINSKI

The narrator of Gustaw Herling-Grudzinski's beautifully crafted, mysterious, and deeply disturbing stories is an elderly Polish writer living in Naples. Ailing and insomniac, he spends his semiretirement as a sort of metaphysical sleuth piecing together accounts of ancient and modern acts of unspeakable evil, awful calamities befalling individuals and communities, outbreaks of cruelty and self-destruction, downfalls of illustrious families, and cases of moral debasement of seemingly stalwart characters. Though hardly enjoying those spectacles of desolation — they sometimes make him physically sick — he seems to be on a personal mission to record some of the devil's more imaginative exploits. The reason for this strange fascination, we are led to believe, is hidden somewhere in his past. From scattered remarks and shards of reminiscences we learn that he was a soldier in World War II, lived through a shattering personal tragedy, and has intimate knowledge of the horrors of the twentieth century.

In these respects, the anonymous protagonist is Herling's narrative double. Gustaw Herling-Grudzinski, as his Polish readers know him, died in 2000 in Naples, where he had spent the larger part of his mature life. He was born in Kielce in 1919, the year Poland entered its independence. He started writing and publishing in high school. In 1937, two years before the outbreak of the war, he enrolled at Warsaw University as a student of Polish literature. During the war he cofounded a clandestine peasant organization, PLAN, and as its emissary tried to sneak to the West in 1940 via Poland's Soviet-occupied eastern lands. He was arrested by the NKVD and charged with espionage for the Germans (apparently the Soviet police did not like his German-sounding name). After enduring the usual tour of several Soviet prisons he ended up in a labor camp near Archangel on the White Sea, where he was sentenced to five years' hard labor. But for a fateful twist of events he, like tens of thousands of other Polish deportees, would likely have disappeared forever in the still-unfathomed vastness of the Gulag Archipelago.

History came to his rescue, though only after his own desperate act of defiance. In 1941 the Germans violated the Ribbentrop-Molotov nonaggression pact and attacked the Soviet Union, which suddenly found itself in need of Western allies. The Polish government in exile negotiated with Stalin the formation of a Polish army made up largely of deportees and political prisoners. Despite the solemn treaty, the fate of prisoners was often the whim of local NKVD officials or camp commanders. Herling volunteered for the Polish army but was denied release. Only after a prolonged, life-threatening hunger strike did he win his freedom. This part of his biography became the subject of his best-known work, *A World Apart*, a fictionalized account of his two years in the Soviet penal system.[1] It was one of the first such literary testimonies, preceding Aleksandr Solzhenitsyn's *One Day in the Life of Ivan Denisovich* by seven years.

Together with his Polish unit, Herling traveled from Soviet

Russia through the Middle East and into Italy. For his valor during the uncommonly bloody and, in the view of some strategists, not-quite-necessary battle of Monte Cassino, he received the highest Polish military distinction, the Order of Virtuti Militari. After the war the author lived first in Rome, then in London, where he finished *A World Apart*. It was also in London that Herling's first wife, the painter Krystyna Domanska, committed suicide. In one of his stories set in that city, the narrator calls London his personal "heart of darkness," a place that gives him attacks of breathlessness and "indefinable fear." From London, he moved to Munich, where he worked as the chief of the cultural department in the Polish section of Radio Free Europe. Finally, in 1955, he moved back to Italy, this time to Naples, where he married the daughter of the Italian philosopher Benedetto Croce.

All that time he wrote and published, in Polish and later also in Italian, stories, literary and art criticism, and political commentaries. He was one of the cofounders and coeditors of the legendary Paris-based Polish magazine *Kultura*, which, during the communist decades, served as the forum of Polish free intellectual life. Though equally at odds with Italian leftist elites and their conservative-Christian counterparts, Herling developed several lifelong friendships among Italy's more independent minds, especially with Ignazio Silone and Nicola Chiaromonte, and wrote for *Il Mondo, Tempo Presente, Il Corriere Della Sera, L'Espresso, Il Giornale, La Stampa*, and other titles. At the same time he kept a highly personal, subtle, meditative diary. It was published during his lifetime as *The Journal Written at Night* and, next to Gombrowicz's *Diary*, is considered one of the greatest examples of Polish memoirist literature.[2] After the fall of communism, Herling frequently visited his native country and became a regular contributor to the newly independent Polish press. His literary reputation in Poland matched that of Czeslaw Milosz, though his feisty, uncompromising views and his declared hostility toward former communists (he refused to call them former), who soon returned to power as so-called social democrats, estranged him even from some former democratic activists.

Herling was equally pugnacious about the policies of the Catholic Church and did not hesitate to criticize Pope John Paul II. In fact, much of his nonpolitical writing seems to be devoted to an angry, passionate, relentless polemic with the Roman Church and its reductive, according to the author, interpretation of the Christian myth. His stories are often constructed as classical mysteries in which the narrator-detective slowly extracts snippets of truth that lie hidden under layers of misleading Christian exegesis.

In the title novella of *The Island: Three Tales*, Sebastiano, a stonemason from an island off the coast of Naples, has a strange accident that leaves him blind and seemingly demented.[3] He escapes from his beautiful wife, Immacolata, and becomes a kind of itinerant hermit isolated from the world by his silence and his incessant, apparently pointless roaming along the rocky paths of the island. Is he simply a weak human being broken by his unexpected, horrible misfortune? Only toward the end of the story, as if reluctant to break the seal of the mystery, the author explains the real nature of Sebastiano's tragedy and shows that its appalling knot of pain, guilt, anger, and shame binds not only him and his wife. Someone else in the island's small community—the least expected of possible actors—is waiting for the miracle of forgiveness and reconciliation. Yet when a miracle of sorts does happen, it looks like another cruel sport of fate played on a helpless and defeated man.

In "The Tower," a Polish soldier recuperating from wounds he received in the Italian campaign of 1945 seeks solitude in a Piedmont village. Fascinated by the life and death of the previous occupant of his house, an elderly schoolteacher, he discovers a striking similarity between his story and the story of the leper of Aosta as told in 1811 by François-Xavier de Maistre. De Maistre's leper friend was confined in a tower on the outskirts of town to live and die in total solitude because of his "unclean" illness. The teacher turned away from the world after the tragic death of his wife and children.

The parallel stories of their lives are a meditation on life without hope, which seems impossible even in the most hopeless of circumstances. In both cases hope does appear to win over resignation. But its victory is also the protagonists' moral defeat. It crushes them and demolishes any structure of integrity they managed to build out of their suffering. The leper of Aosta, seemingly reconciled with his fate, has a moment of soul-destroying weakness when life appears to offer him a glimmer of hope. And after years of rejecting life, the teacher from Piedmont breaks down while facing execution by the Nazis and unwittingly sends another man to his death.

The last and most enigmatic of the three stories in *The Island* is "The Second Coming." Set in thirteenth-century Orvieto, it tells of the last year in the life of Pope Urban IV, a skillful, unscrupulous politician and one of the architects of the Church's earthly power. But the author portrays him in his infirmity, in a dominion beleaguered by plague, apostasy, and religious madness. Insomniac and ill, the aged pope is losing his faith and plaintively waiting for a sign from God.

Two related events disturb his meditative seclusion in Orvieto. One of them is the torment and death of a young priest from Bolsena who doubted the presence of Christ in the Eucharist. Charged with apostasy, he died a horrible death — first praying, then cursing God — in an iron cage suspended from Torre del Papa (the Pope's Tower) in Orvieto. A few days later, according to fervent witnesses, as if to prove the guilt of the doubting cleric, blood started dripping from a consecrated Host in nearby Bolsena. The pope, who has watched the death of the priest with seeming indifference, acknowledges "the miracle of Bolsena" but despite the demands of the crowd refuses to recognize it as a harbinger of the Second Coming of Christ.

A year later, as Urban lies on his deathbed, his glance falls on a verse from the New Testament: "Then Jesus, aware that everything was accomplished, in order to fulfill the scripture, cried 'I thirst.'" The pope remembers he has heard that phrase in his dream uttered by the dying priest. The author leaves the reader to ponder whether we should take this simple plea for human compassion for Christ's true message that has been lost among the religious fervor and Church politics of the "Christian era," or for a resigned admission that our spiritual thirst will never be satiated and will always lead us to love and blasphemy, to acts of sainthood as well as to acts of unimaginable cruelty.

In these stories of loneliness, doubt, and life suspended between despair and hope, one can clearly hear the echo of the author's own experiences as a prisoner, a soldier, and an exile. While weaving them, in his elegant, Stendhalian prose into the timeless narrative of human anguish, he never allows the reader to forget about the physical reality of pain. He certainly refers to something much closer in time than the Middle Ages when he writes of "Jews and heretics" being burned at the stake of collective insanity. Likewise, it is not literature but personal memory that we hear in his calling life "a dream of death, in a tower surrounded by the sea, from which one is awakened by an unfathomable spasm of fright only at the approach of actual death."

In many of Herling's stories the Italian landscape, with its stunning beauty and its desiccated hardness, seems to scorn the "moist" human drama. But it also cleanses and depersonalizes, like a classical ancient tragedy, and even provides the narrator with something akin to consolation. As in Zbigniew Herbert's poetry, the visible and the palpable — landscapes, stones, the useful and beautiful objects created by man — are always there whenever the spectator is ready to avert his eyes from the murky interior of the human soul. One of his characters, seeking refuge from the memories of war, remarks in *The Island*, "Since the world has been, someone has always fallen only to be lifted in arms of mercy; since the beginning, the sea has patiently washed away the blood of the dead, the moon has imperturbably illuminated the houses of the living deep in sleep, while the sunlashed island rests and refreshes itself in the arms of the night. How to repel that world and withdraw from it forever?"

But in his next collection of stories published in English, *The Noonday Cemetery*, the author seems to reject even this frail affirmation.[4] Most of his protagonists as well as the narrator are drawn to dark, narrow, gloomy places—a gorge at the foot of a mountain, a cave, catacomb cities, monastic cells, old, unaired mansions. The author often employs a strange reversal of settings, with death taking place in the sun while life that precedes it unfolds in darkness.

One of the most disturbing stories in the volume is "Beata, Santa," which touched off a controversy in Poland because it was interpreted as an attack on Pope John Paul II's uncompromising antiabortion stance. "Beata, Santa" tells the story of Marianna, a young Polish girl who pays an ill-fated visit to the former Yugoslavia on the eve of the outbreak of the savage ethnic war in Bosnia. Captured by Bosnian Serbs, she ends up in one of the "rape camps" for Bosnian women. She gets pregnant, but after her release she decides to honor the pope's appeal to raped women and not have an abortion.

The Church seizes the opportunity and starts a propaganda campaign, presenting the pious, meek Marianna as a model of Christian womanhood. What is most mystifying is that the girl seems truly pure, spiritually untouched by her terrifying experiences, and full of love for God, for people, and for the child she is carrying. A kindly Italian priest who offers her shelter (she is reluctant to return to Poland) starts to spread rumors about her saintly qualities. When the girl dies in childbirth—

serene and acquiescent — the Church immediately begins her beatification process. And then . . . a horrifying discovery is made. In an exceptionally cruel way, fate seems to mock the young woman, the Church zealots, and all their naive attempts to turn a story of unparalleled evil into an edifying tale of triumphant Christian virtue.

After the publication of the story, Herling admitted that he was aggravated by the pope's appeal to raped women. "I thought it was very unjust — terrible," he said in an interview. Yet "Beata, Santa" is much more than a polemic against the smugness and hypocrisy of organized religion. Like most other stories in the volume, it touches upon something ambiguous and impenetrable that Herling finds at the core of every great act of evil. His narrator is attracted to this forbidden zone and yet recoils from it in horror. We never learn, for example, what hides behind Marianna's angelic demeanor. The narrator thinks he may know — he has heard her talking in her dreams — but he is too disturbed to tell. It also seems that the evil done to Marianna by people, horrific as it is, may be only a tiny splinter of some extrahuman, one might say cosmic, evil that wishes to destroy everything that makes her a person.

Similar puzzles appear in almost all of Herling's stories: a missing chapter, a lost document, an unreliable witness, a fact too strange or ominous to recount. In the title story, the narrator investigates the double suicide, or the murder and suicide, of a pair of unlikely lovers. He is traumatized less by their fate than by the anonymity and inexplicability of their death. In "The Height of Summer," a scrupulous captain of the Roman police tries to get to the bottom of an epidemic of suicides that descends upon his city each year around August 15. At the end, however, he must seal his report with "a large question mark in the middle of the page." In "The Silver Coffer," a document containing a confession of incest and murder by a sixteenth-century aristocrat and monk crumbles into pieces before the narrator has a chance to read much of it. He tries to recreate it from the few readable scraps, aware that he merely creates his own fantasy of the events: "At the most there were two or three words here and there, which allowed one to speculate, and stimulated the imagination, forming the separated spans of a ruined bridge across an abyss of silence." A ruined life, the author seems to suggest, is like a ruined edifice: It stirs imagination and provokes speculations but conceals its original, obliterated form.

In some stories in *The Noonday Cemetery* the author plays with the convention of the gothic tale. There are visions on the border of waking and dreaming, demonic possessions, exorcisms, inanimate objects that seem to have a hidden life. There is even an apparition that steps out of an old portrait to deliver a hearty kick to a trembling witness. Those deliberate pastiches suggest that the author takes his own fascination with evil and death with a bit of irony. Sometimes his characters engage in arcane disputes on the origin and nature of evil. "The Eyetooth of Barabbas" is founded on a heretical-Gnostic theory that God needed evil to make his creation complete. According to the story, it is the obscure bandit Barabbas rather than the allegedly renegade disciple Judas who plays the bête noire of the Christian myth. Judas is merely a tool in God's hands, and he is punished for his preordained treason. Barabbas, by contrast, appears to be entirely free in his evildoing, totally dismissive of Christ and his teachings. And he seems to leave the story unpunished—perhaps even triumphant? Is he, as his abnormal eyetooth may suggest, a stand-in for the devil himself?

Herling likes to toy with philosophical and theological interpretations of evil, but eventually he casts them away as inadequate or disingenuous. He is not interested in solving the perennial puzzle but rather in showing how the puzzle blends into the landscape of daily human affairs, how it colors human ambitions, hopes, and fears, and how skillfully it evades all attempts to rationalize it. The secret of evil, says Herling, is so old and so persistent that it has become an integral part—as a secret—of our humanity. We can no more understand it than we can vanquish it in this world.

Herling's writing is both deeply religious and fiercely antireligious—like an atheist's constant wrestling with God. When a longing for transcendence or a longing for God becomes religion, the author seems to suggest, it turns against its own nature. It starts to present itself as a solution instead of a question, certainty instead of doubt. For Herling, faith, if taken seriously enough and far enough, does not make life easier but crushes it with its burden. It is a paradox more likely to warp and corrupt lives than save and reinforce them. The paradox of faith is best exemplified in the book of Job, to which Herling frequently returns in his stories and memoirs. Job must love and worship God, who is "a Lord blinded by His own omnipotence, who demands that man seek justice in His amorality, since in His divine omniscience He does not know what human suffering is." Total faith, says Herling, "entails a theological suspension of morality." It is a form of madness that frequently spills into secular life, wrecks individual lives and whole communities.

It seems that Herling's heroes face only two possibilities: religious inertia or religious frenzy. In *Volcano and Miracle* he addresses the dilemma directly: "But authentic religion, like authentic freedom, means ceaseless questioning, more even, the ceaseless doubting of living souls. Certainty exists only among the ranks of the disciplined, the servile and deceptive of dead souls." Servility and certitude lead to spiritual death; feverish searching may lead to sainthood, but more often it leads to the loss of simple human empathy. The more intense the faith, the closer to blasphemy and madness.

Can people, who dwell so deeply in contradictions, occasionally enjoy the light of reason and beauty? The stories in *The Noonday Cemetery*, written in the last years of the author's life, may at first seem morbid and obsessive. And yet, through the force of Herling's dispassionate prose, there is something beautiful, even uplifting in those parables about people at their limits, in total isolation, at a point where they have to decide whether to reject life or, despite everything they know, affirm it. They are like the people in *Volcano and Miracle* whose village has been obliterated by an earthquake: "They stood motionless, like stone, they seldom spoke, and when they did the words were like shreds torn from lumped throats. Their eyes had a cold numb intensity, as if they were looking at something for the last time: it went beyond the bounds of suffering, to where despair turns to indifference."

In the face of such loss, abject resignation and stubborn hope seem equally justified. At least that is what Herling's detached voice seems to suggest. But he also knows which of these options is more likely to prevail. As he suggests in "The Tower," humans without hope would be incomplete. They will cling to hope despite the fact that hope will often lead them astray and confuse their moral judgment. Hope is, for Herling, the most ambiguous of the three cardinal Christian virtues. In *Volcano and Miracle* he quotes two known authorities on hopelessness. Polish writer and Auschwitz concentration camp survivor Tadeusz Borowski, the author of *This Way to the Gas, Ladies and Gentlemen*, wrote, "Never in the history of mankind was hope stronger, and never did it bring such wickedness as it did in this war, this camp. We were not taught to reject hope, therefore we die in gas chambers." Varlam Shalamov of *The Kolyma Tales* spoke in strikingly similar terms of his experiences in the Soviet Gulag: "Hope is always a shackle for a prisoner. Hope is always a slavery. The man with hope will change his behavior for anything, he acts wickedly more often than the man without hope." But liberating oneself from that "slavery" may be beyond human power. Just as true religion leads Herling's protagonists to blasphemy, and blasphemy sometimes leads them back to God, hope brings them to destitution, which in turn generates something that can almost be taken for hope — a tenacity, a violent resistance to emptiness that may be the "indestructible hard kernel of humanity" Kafka spoke about. "When it comes down to it, what is hope?" asks Herling. "Impotent rebellion against despair. Whoever says that one can't live without hope is simply asserting that one cannot live without constant rebellion."

Strange as it may sound, with the passing of time the Polish tragedy of decades spent under communism looks more and more like a grotesque. When young Polish writers decide to venture into the pre-Solidarity past, they almost invariably choose a comic rather than a tragic style. What strikes one today, from a safe distance, as hopelessly comic is a certain asymmetry between the two sides that faced each other, especially in the last decades of decaying totalitarianism. On one side — the opposition with its fervent idealism, readiness to sacrifice, lofty, romantic rhetoric; on the other — vulgarity, shabbiness, boredom, pettiness, an enemy whose emissaries looked increasingly haggard, bumbling, grungy, almost pitiful. Yes, the system could still bite, but its teeth were rotten. Encounters with the enemy instilled a feeling of repulsion rather than fear.

As long as communism held sway in Poland, very few people wanted to talk about this slightly farcical aspect of the experience. Neither did Polish literature. Unlike Russians and Czechs with their highly developed sense of the ridiculous and the absurd, Poles under communism seemed stuck in the language of solemn exhortations and lofty gestures. One of the few exceptions was Tadeusz Konwicki, who managed to capture the uncanny mood of the final years of communism in his novels and his nonfiction writing. The system in his novels appears less as a coercive tyranny than as a black hole warping and demeaning every dream and desire, every higher striving of the human spirit.

Konwicki, a prolific novelist as well as an accomplished film director and screenwriter, was born in 1926 in Nowa Wilejka, near Wilno, in what was then the Polish-controlled part of Lithuania. He grew up in a country still living in the pastoral past — a country whose folklore and collective memory reached back to the Middle Ages. Like his older countryman Czeslaw Milosz, whose autobiographical novel he made into a film shortly before the declaration of martial law in Poland, he inherited an acute sense of historical destiny, a belief in the magical power of national dreams, and a taste for visionary realism.

During the war, Konwicki was deported to Germany as a forced laborer but managed to escape and return to his native region. He joined the resistance Home Army at a time when, after the expulsion of the Germans by the Soviets, Lithuania became a bitter battleground for various political and military forces, including Polish and Lithuanian nationalists, Soviet security forces, former Nazi collaborators, and bands of common criminals. According to his scattered reminiscences, he did take part in some anticommunist operations, but, seeing the futility of continuing bloodshed, he "deserted" his detachment and moved to Poland. For awhile he studied literature at the Yagiellonian University in Krakow and at Warsaw University and screenwriting at the newly established Film School in Lodz. He never graduated, however, and soon started publishing fiction and journalism and assisting several prominent Polish film directors. One of his early films, a short, low-budget feature called *The Last Day of Summer* (1958), prefigured the austere stylistics of French New Wave cinema. It tells the story of a young man and a young woman who meet by chance on a Baltic beach. Despite being attracted to each other, their attempts to communicate and establish an emotional bond fail because of their harrowing wartime memories. Though shot mostly in bright, opens spaces, the atmosphere of the film is dark and claustrophobic. We never learn what really happened to each of them during the war, but the shadow of the past is almost physically present in every scene.

Despite his anticommunist past, Konwicki followed the path of many in his generation in trying to reconcile himself with the new regime. He joined the Communist Party and became a member of a group of young literary enthusiasts of the new power. His first stories and articles exalted the heroic workers involved in the "construction of socialism," and his first published novel, *Power* (1954), followed the official model of socialist realism.[1] Like the majority of Poles with similar biographies, however, he soon became disillusioned with the communist state. As a writer, he decided to follow his own vision of the times and events he had witnessed. In 1963 he published *A Dreambook for Our Time*, a novel that established his literary reputation.[2] It was also the first of Konwicki's works to make full use of his ability to find the fantastic among the quotidian and to transform the familiar landscapes of late-communist Poland into a surreal setting of the perennial Polish drama of futility. In this particular novel, the story is of a motley group of people repatriated from the now-Soviet areas who learn that their new settlement will soon be flooded by a dam.

In most of Konwicki's novels, starting with *A Dreambook*, there exists a characteristic reversal of temporal grounds. The remembered past — personal or collective, idyllic or horrible — is clear, vivid, and presented in a realist mode, while the present, the novelistic here and now, has a surreal, otherworldly quality. Time appears to move in circles or split into alternative strands. It is as if the narrator-protagonist, usually resembling Konwicki himself, doubted that his world — postwar Poland — exists as an actual reality and not as a figment of his unhinged mind. Perhaps the most extreme examples of that approach are Konwicki's two novels, a fairy-tale/fantasy *The Anthropos-Spectre-Beast* and *The Ascension*, in which the amnesiac (or maybe dead) protagonist wanders the streets of nighttime Warsaw, mysteriously drawn by a bizarre Warsaw landmark — the Stalinist skyscraper known as the Palace of Culture and Science.[3]

The unreality of the present, the images of crumbling and decay, the progressing sense of loss and mental deterioration of the protagonists, and the ominous shadow of the Big Neighbor, the Soviet Union, were clear allusions to the state of Polish society in the late 1960s and 1970s. Konwicki's works were clothed in the Aesopian, though easily recognizable, symbolic language and partly hidden behind the fantastic deformation of the setting, but they were among the most powerful literary attempts to capture the dark farce of the times.

In 1966 the writer made a fateful personal choice. He signed an open letter protesting the expulsion from the party of the prominent Polish philosopher Leszek Kolakowski. The expulsion was the result of an official campaign against party "revisionists," people who advocated a more humanistic variant of

Marxism and a more liberal course for the communist state. As a result of his outspokenness, Konwicki, too, was expelled from the party, though he was permitted to continue publishing and making films. As the political atmosphere in Poland became more stifling in the 1970s, he drifted closer and closer to the new democratic opposition. When, in 1977, a group of Polish dissidents established a semiclandestine publishing network called Nowa, Konwicki was one of the first writers to send them a manuscript, his novel *The Polish Complex*, soon followed by *A Minor Apocalypse*.[4] Both books became major events in the Polish alternative culture circles that started to flourish after the formation of the Committee for the Defense of Workers (KOR) and other informal dissident groups. But they also provoked controversy because some found Konwicki's treatment of the most cherished national myths and of the young opposition insufficiently reverential.

Now beyond the reach of official censorship and no longer needing to hide his political allusions behind elaborate literary tropes, the author kept nevertheless his characteristic surreal style. If anything, his plots became even more bizarre, the settings even more fantastic, and his protagonists even more uncertain of their purpose and identity. Like Konwicki's earlier novels, *The Polish Complex* moves back and forth between the carefully reconstructed historical past — this time the Polish anti-Russian uprising of 1863 — and the familiar absurdities of contemporary Polish life. The story brings together a mixed, yet typical, group of Poles from the early 1970s: disenchanted intellectuals, tired workers, police informers, con men, communist careerists — all observed by the narrator and the main character, the Polish writer Tadeusz Konwicki. The characters meet while waiting in line outside an empty jewelry shop that is supposed to receive a shipment of Russian gold rings. In the faltering Polish economy gold rings were considered a relatively safe way of preserving one's life savings. And waiting in a queue was an almost perfect metaphor of life under communism. A queue reflected the tedium and apathy, the total dependence upon the centrally distributed goods, superficial egalitarianism, and the plethora of secret codes about acceptable and unacceptable forms of cheating.

Very little happens on the surface of the novel. People are stranded on a chilly Warsaw street. It is Christmas Eve, and they all wish they were somewhere else — with their relatives and friends. Yet they have suspended their real lives for the vague promise of a trifling material reward. They quarrel, reminisce, and try to trick their way closer to the empty counter. Some of them sneak out to a nearby dive where an invalid war hero serves illegal vodka while a band of street musicians is rehearsing Christmas carols.

One of the men in line, the proud owner of an American visa and a plane ticket, introduces himself as Tadeusz Kojran, the fictive Konwicki's former comrade-in-arms in the Home Army, who after the war was ordered by a secret organization to execute the writer for desertion and collaboration with the communist government. With him is a fat ex-policeman called Duszek (in Polish meaning "little spirit" or "brownie"), who apparently arrested Kojran many years ago during the time of the Stalinist purges and tortured him in prison. Later he clung to his victim like an old buddy, waiting in vain for absolution.

There are others: a young plainclothesman who models himself on American cops from the movies, a French anarchist who wants to become a Polish citizen, a peasant woman who turns out to be the heiress to an American fortune, a beautiful shop assistant called, interchangeably, Iwona and Basia (we never learn her real name), who is seduced by Konwicki in the shop's staff room.

As the group waits, several Soviet tourists arrive. They too want to buy gold rings. They are friendly and polite yet take for granted their right to go to the head of the line. One of them is recognized by the narrator as Kaziuk, a relative from his native Lithuania and now a content worker on a collective farm. He happens to have with him a family memento, a stone seal used by a nineteenth-century Polish insurrectionist in a penal colony in Siberia. Finally, instead of gold rings the customers are offered cheap electric samovars with a special bonus — the chance of winning a trip to the Soviet Union. Ironically, the prize goes to Kojran, who was about to depart for America, leaving him in a quandary about his destination.

As the people gradually reveal their life stories — with Konwicki as their medium, their confessor, as well as an offstage commenting voice — it becomes clear that their failures and frustrations have deeper roots than the everyday hardships and humiliations of postwar Polish life. Most of them, like the narrator Konwicki himself, are tormented by a real or irrational sense of guilt, by feelings of utter uselessness, and the wish for death. "Listen to what happened to me, Konwa," says Kojran. "I was once a boy from a fairy-tale. I was Janek the musician, the sorcerer's apprentice, a young Byron. How did I hit the skids? What was the mix-up that left me a primitive old codger? Must have been my lack of training. My consciousness, my perception system, my sensibility, the tendons of my soul, the lenses of my clairvoyance, they all remained dormant. I never practiced or perfected or encouraged any of it. And that's why it withered away and died in me before I was even dead myself. I condemned myself to an animal existence. Or could that have been fate?"

Something went wrong in the lives of these people — a long time ago or just recently — something involving not only individuals but also the Polish community as a whole. An act of betrayal was committed — Konwicki muses — yet no one wanted to be a betrayer. A destiny was sabotaged, yet no one was clear what the destiny was. What, then, is the real source of the agony of Konwicki's characters?

A kind of answer can be found in the historical plot of the novel that interweaves with the contemporary one. One of the episodes concerns Zygmunt Mineyko, an ill-fated young soldier who, toward the end of the uprising of 1863 — probably the most tragic and mismanaged in the long sequence of hopeless Polish uprisings — tries to organize a partisan unit in Lithuania. Another is the story of a historical figure, Romuald Traugutt, a former officer in the Russian army and a Polish patriot who is appointed the "dictator" of the same uprising in its final, hopeless phase.

Both men throw themselves into the struggle when the chances for victory are practically nonexistent. Popular zeal has burned out, and Russian repressions have paralyzed the civilian population. Mineyko, left without arms, money, or support, continues to train a handful of enthusiastic but ill-prepared youths, who disperse and go home when the first shot is fired in a trifling encounter. Mineyko is betrayed by peasants, who turn him over to the Russians. Traugutt, after taking leave of his wife, heads for Warsaw to assume his post, although he knows that the entire patriotic movement had been infiltrated — some say controlled — by agents of the Russian secret police and that his arrest and execution are imminent. Both heroes accept their fate with courage and resignation, as if obeying historical compulsions older and less comprehensible than the patriotic slogans they repeat. They cannot change their destiny because they feel they are in fact apparitions from a beautiful, terrifying dream dreamt for generations by crushed, hopeless people like those passively waiting in front of the jewelry shop.

Trapped for centuries in a political deadlock, the Polish people have lived with a sense of thwarted ambitions and political failure. Since history itself provided little hope, their will to survive took an ahistorical, apolitical form — a romance of unique spiritual Polishness and something that Konwicki calls a "religion of freedom." It boiled down to the unshakable belief in an ultimate liberation and the fulfillment of all national longings, past, present, and future, the promise of a final national redemption that will take place perhaps here, on earth, and perhaps in some higher, metaphysical realm.

Like most religions, the Polish "religion of freedom" proved to be a source of astonishing moral power in times of crisis, yet it also created its own orthodoxy. It instilled in its followers an overwhelming sense of guilt and demanded a constant ritual of sacrifice. Nowhere was its presence more clearly demonstrated than in the tradition of Polish insurgency. The "Romantic Uprisings" — a term used by Polish historians not only for the repeated attempts at liberation during the nineteenth century but also for the horrific Warsaw Uprising against the German occupiers in 1944 — usually started as military ventures based on political calculations and a sense of attainable goals. Yet after the rebels ran up against the overwhelming force of the enemy or faced a political stalemate preventing them from reaching their goal, their struggles turned into a burnt offering meant to transform physical defeat into moral victory, to create a legend that would take hold of future generations. For external observers the spectacle was often inexplicable and offensive, but Poles perceived it as the only strategy of spiritual survival.

However, the romantic dream had also a negative side. Born of a sense of failure, it included failure as a part of its mythology. It marked bold political undertakings with a certain fatalism and extremism and tended to undermine limited, yet realistic projects. After some time the sarcophagi of national martyrdom started to issue the poisons of hatred and frustrations. The irresistible force of the national will crashing against a wall of historical impossibility left behind the sour heat of wasted energy and inaction.

The contemporary plot of *The Polish Complex* portrays this final phase of the Polish historical cycle. The characters gathered on Christmas Eve — for Poles, a time of remembrance and hope — represent different forms of moral decomposition and failure. Yet at the same time these people seem the wretched children of such heroes as Mineyko and Traugutt. Their thoughts and drunken confessions recall the same romantic creed, debased and caricatured as they are, like the slogans about the uniqueness of the Polish character mouthed by Duszek and the half-obliterated words "Honor and Fatherland," the battle cry of the Polish knighthood, tattooed on the arm of Kojran, who dreams now only about inheriting a gas station in America.

Hence, "was it worth it?"—the inevitable question uttered by Mineyko as he is taken to be executed—resounds in the contemporary story of *The Polish Complex*. Did the tradition of resistance and sacrifice confer upon the Poles special spiritual powers, as they themselves like to believe? or is the Polish fate "a fate which causes degeneration, like every misfortune, every calamity"? The character of the people waiting for gold on a December night seems to point to the latter option. Yet was any alternative overlooked or ignored?

The history presented in *The Polish Complex* has a déjà vu quality. It is experienced as a cycle, repeating itself with striking regularity. At one point, as if talking to the ghost of Mineyko, Konwicki recalls his own involvement in the partisan struggle toward the end of the Second World War:

And before you, just as it would be before me half a century later, lay the future—unknown, mysterious, majestic. Our unknowable fate, the country's Golgotha. A hot, sultry hope; an inspiring, ardent premonition. You were twenty-three years old. You were five years older than I, and eighty years younger. . . .

What were we thinking about on the invisible threshold of time? Ourselves? Poland? I don't remember anymore and I don't know how to summon it up from the past now dead or rather fixed forever, those moments of inconceivable self-enchantment and humility, audacity and fear, greedy hope and foolhardy uncertainty. In just the same way I do not know how to summon back that Poland which we bore within ourselves like the overwhelming pain of the first spasm of a coronary.

New actors come on stage to pick up the same familiar script. The choice of roles is, as usual, a limited one: Hero, Skeptic, Traitor. Such a disturbing vision of history poses the question of what ultimate human or metaphysical sense it may make. This question hovers over the events presented in *The Polish Complex*, and although no answer is given, the people in line continue to wait for an answer. Konwicki the writer persists in his search: "I write because in my subconscious there stirs a spark of hope that somewhere there is something, that something endures somewhere, that, in my last instant, Great Meaning will take notice of me and save me from a universe without meaning." So do the people freezing on a Warsaw street. At the end of the book the line refuses to disperse even when it becomes clear that the gold rings will not be delivered. The pointless vigil becomes a symbol of the eternal Polish wake, a wait for a miracle of understanding and rebirth.

Before it happens, however, the sense of meaninglessness and futility that chills the hapless line of people in *The Polish Complex* is given full rein in Konwicki's next novel, *A Minor Apocalypse*, a futuristic tragic farce published in Poland in 1979. The place is unmistakably Warsaw; the time, some indefinite future, although we are allowed to guess that we are well beyond Orwell's 1984. The world is falling apart both physically and morally. Houses and bridges collapse, shops are empty, money loses value, cars run on buttermilk. Even time deteriorates. There are no calendars, so nobody can tell the date. Seasons of the year blur and merge. Life is a grotesque, sometimes hilarious, yet always terrifying spectacle of decay and degradation. The process evidently has been a long and gradual one, since nobody seems to notice or care. In fact, people have adapted to their subhuman condition pretty well. Even a diminishing group of dissidents, disillusioned about their activities, which are manipulated and corrupted by the regime, provides little hope for the future.

This is the background against which the protagonist-narrator Konwicki wakes up in the morning with an undeserved hangover (he had not been drinking the previous night) and, like Kafka's Joseph K., is unexpectedly visited by two strangers. The two men, named Hubert and Rysio, demand that at eight o'clock that very night he commit suicide in front of Central Party Headquarters. Time is of the essence because precisely at that hour Poland will officially cease to be. It will join the Soviet Union as yet another "socialist republic." Konwicki's task is to make "the elevated, the majestic, the holy" gesture to shake people in Poland and elsewhere. The two messengers explain that he, Konwicki, is the only person suitable for such a sacrifice. He is a known writer, one whose death will cause some stir, yet not important enough to be a significant loss to Polish culture. Besides, his private obsession with death, clearly present in his fiction, makes him a perfect candidate for heroic self-annihilation.

Konwicki rejects the proposition as senseless and cynical, although he takes it quite seriously. He leaves his house with the intention of sneaking out of his assignment at the last moment.

Yet he is immediately caught in a web of strange events that seems to push him relentlessly toward his fate. It looks as if his steps followed some hidden pattern outlined by agents more powerful than he and his morning visitors. His apparently aimless peregrinations along the dilapidated streets of Warsaw become stages of yet another personal Golgotha and a ritual of reckoning on the eve of the nation's apocalypse. Similarly, his internal monologue, in which he tries to negate the sense of any sacrifice in a world like his, paradoxically becomes the justification of that sacrifice. In the last scene of the book we see him, still with a hangover, climbing the steps of the Palace of Culture and Science (the place of his anticipated self-immolation has been changed to a site well known from Konwicki's other novels) with a can of gasoline and a box of Swedish matches provided conscientiously by his friends.

When the novel was first published in Poland, it was met with bewilderment and more than a few voices of protest. *A Minor Apocalypse* is a roman à clef, portraying in a thinly veiled way several well-known figures from official as well as underground culture and politics. Many people took personal offense. Konwicki seemed to be bent on settling accounts with just about everybody: the Russians, the West, the government, the opposition, the intellectuals, the artists, and his countrymen in general. Konwicki's fantasy was interpreted as a report on the actual state of affairs in the country. As such, it seemed grossly exaggerated and one-sided. Some critics charged the author with being ignorant of the real political mechanisms and with lacking in appreciation for the transformative power and the determination of Polish workers — objections that were borne out by the sudden rise of Solidarity in 1980, which woke up the apathetic society.

But such an approach misses the point. Konwicki is definitely not a political writer. He is an explorer of the Polish collective subconscious. He is interested in the subjective reality of a people crippled by fate, banished from the world of normal social pursuits and achievements into the domain of dreams, myths, and futile expectations. Using his own biography as archetypal for his generation, he explores the ways in which Poles create, transform, and destroy their symbols, how they turn their weaknesses into strengths and their strengths into weaknesses. The characters that appear in his novels are real people as well as phantoms from the narrator's past and emblematic figures from the Polish collective consciousness. "The boy from the provinces" who accompanies the protagonist and who turns out to be a police informer may also be the author's alter ego (his name is also Tadeusz) or his lost youth. The famous writer and Konwicki's master, Jan, who had almost reached Parnassus and now is drinking himself to death in his Warsaw apartment, perhaps modeled on Jerzy Andrzejewski, the author of *Ashes and Diamonds*, represents the Polish striving to be admitted to the family of great European cultures. There is also a paralyzed soldier of the Home Army, who follows the disintegration of his country on a TV screen, and a mysterious Russian girl, Nadezhda, who seems to represent Poland's secret fascination with its Russian neighbor and frequent oppressor.

History in this world is experienced as a repeated disaster or a continuous ending. Konwicki's heroes see their universe evaporating into nothingness, and they in turn are forced out of their familiar domains. By placing his story in an indefinite future, where time has almost ceased to exist (the government has stopped printing calendars, each clock shows a different hour), Konwicki captures this repetitive character of the Polish drama, giving us not Poland in a particular moment but a summa of Polish history. What we see is happening right now, has happened before, and will happen again. History seemed to confirm Konwicki's predictions when the military crackdown against Solidarity in December 1981 temporarily destroyed all hopes for a major political breakthrough.

Yet there is something even more ominous and terminal in the world of *A Minor Apocalypse*. The novel is also a vision of totalitarianism in the final stage of its decay, which may be, as the author seems to suggest, the state of its final victory. The most terrifying aspect of this kind of totalitarianism is its almost absolute transparence — "slavery covered by a sloppy coat of contemporary polish," as Konwicki's hero remarks. Those who insist on measuring oppression by the number of political prisoners, the degree of police coercion, and the effectiveness of governmental control would find there little reason for indignation. True, there is poverty and corruption of grotesque proportions, yet they are hardly restricted to the totalitarian world. There is also the secret police, which tortures the main hero in a highly inventive, "scientific" way. Still, it looks almost like a relic from the good old days of real struggle and sharp divisions between "us" and "them." In reality, the regime itself has grown senile and weak. Its functions have become merely ritualistic. People are mostly left alone, allowed to pursue their petty ambitions. Watched from a safe distance, they may almost seem free. They make money, sign petitions, and take part in protests; then they get drunk and have a good time, like Rysio; they can even write plotless, modernistic novels that use neither punctuation nor dialogue. Yet they are slaves, and their slavery has an utterly unprecedented dimension. There is a lot of movement, a lot of happening in this world, yet there is no progress. The slavery in Konwicki's novel results from the fact that some great, universal striving that has accompanied humanity throughout its history has irreversibly ended.

The secret power of totalitarianism, Konwicki tells us, is its tremendous inertia, which is triggered perhaps by some historical mistake and which drives the system to its grim conclusion. Its ultimate result may be the death of history itself, the living, mostly unnoticed death of the world: "This city is the capital of a people evaporating into nothingness. Something needs to be said about that, too. But to whom?"

The world has gotten used to much more spectacular versions of the apocalypse, and Konwicki, like so many writers from the communist world, warns us that the true apocalypse may come in the form of "an Antichrist diluted, broken into bits and granules," which can be swallowed, easily overlooked. *A Minor Apocalypse* is clearly an exercise in extreme pessimism, but even Konwicki stops short of total hopelessness. When the crippled soldier of the Home Army points to the dying world, the narrator suddenly protests:

"The world can't die. Many generations have thought that the world was dying. But it was only their world which was dying."

"Well said. But if the world isn't dying, then you have to live somehow."

"What does that mean?"

"That means you need to have a human death."

Konwicki's protagonist clings to a belief in the immortality of the world, and this belief makes him accept his own, seemingly absurd death as the only human conclusion of the day of humiliations and reckonings. But is his death a real act of sacrifice meant to redeem and save some value for the future? The hero, with his irony and taste for dialectical negations, does not give a clear answer. He goes to his death as confused and doubting as when he left home in the morning. Is he following in the footsteps of Mineyko and Traugutt by assuming, even against himself, the eternal role of the Polish Martyr? Is his act a case of eschatological rebellion against the impersonal forces of history — a proof that a human being can be truly free only by committing something entirely absurd and gratuitous? The list of possible answers can go on. But there is something eerily Polish about the figure of an ironist and a skeptic assuming in the end the role of a hero and a martyr.

History has added an unexpected postscript to both of Konwicki's novels. Not long after the publication of *A Minor Apocalypse* the rise of Solidarity suddenly restored the currency of the myth of Polish romantic insurrectionism. A year and a half later, General Wojciech Jaruzelski's martial law again left Poles waiting in the cold. Tadeusz Konwicki was one of the first writers arrested in the roundup on the first night of the crackdown. The old scenario was playing out, scene after scene, trapping people in the fixed pattern of familiar gestures and responses. Then came the year 1989, when communism simply ended, and the old vicious circle of Polish history finally seemed to have been broken. But has it, really? A whole new generation of Poles grew up knowing communism from hearsay, just as my generation knew World War II. But the ghosts of Poland's past continue to haunt the collective subconscious. They surface unexpectedly during every election, every crisis. During daily frustrations with the economy, corruption, social ills, during debates about Poland's relations with Germany, Russia, Europe, and America, the public debate can reach unexpected emotional intensity, as if some powerful enemy were at the gates and everything was again at stake. What makes Polish politics still more about the past than about the future? What makes Polish moods swing between smugness and hopelessness? What makes them set out on crusades to save Europe's soul and stand in endless lines (the only ones left) to get "tourist" visas to America? At least some answers to those questions can be found in Konwicki's books — those still-unsurpassed catalogs of the "hypnotic phantoms" of the Polish mind.

ADAM ZAGAJEWSKI

In the title poem of his volume *Mysticism for Beginners*,[1] Adam Zagajewski takes us to Montepulciano, one of Tuscany's fabled hill-towns, where, among the usual splendors of such places (the dusk "erasing the outlines of medieval houses," "olive trees on little hills," "stained-glass windows like butterfly wings"), he suddenly declares his belief that the world given to our senses is not all there is, that any landscape

> and any journey, any kind of trip,
> are only mysticism for beginners,
> the elementary course, prelude
> to a test that's been
> postponed

The phrase "mysticism for beginners," the poem explains, was inspired by a book of this title spotted in the lap of a German tourist, possibly another New Age guide to higher spiritual awareness. The contrast between the poet's solemn declaration of a mystical premise and the lowly context in which the word "mysticism" appears in the poem points to the central question of Zagajewski's poetry: Can metaphysical inquiry still be a rightful concern of poetry in our profoundly skeptical and ironic culture? or, to reverse the question, can serious poetry survive without metaphysical mystery and ecstasy? can it be sustained by irony alone, which the poet calls, in "Long Afternoons," "the gaze / that sees but doesn't penetrate"?

Zagajewski, well known to American readers for both his poetry and his essays, may seem an unlikely candidate to raise such questions. He belongs to what is known as Poland's Solidarity generation, that particular breed of tough, down-to-earth dreamers and pragmatic romantics born at the end of or right after World War II who made ironic defiance their weapon of choice against totalitarian, ideological rant.

The poet was born in 1945 in Lvov, today's Lviv, which before the war was a predominantly Polish city in the heart of Polish-controlled Galicia, today Western Ukraine. After the war the area became part of the Soviet Socialist Republic of Ukraine, and the Zagajewski family had to relocate to Gliwice, formerly German Gleiwitz, in Upper Silesia, which was assigned to Poland as compensation for its "Eastern Lands" incorporated by the Soviet Union. Those movements of borders and people, combined with the imposition of the alien, unwelcome communist system, contributed to the sense of dislocation and nomadic impermanence that characterized the first decades of the postwar era in Poland.

After graduating from high school, Zagajewski moved once again, this time to Krakow, where he attended the Yagellonian University, one of the oldest schools in this part of Europe. Later in life he lived in Paris and Houston and finally returned to Krakow, following in the footsteps of the dean of Polish poetry, Czeslaw Milosz. In his autobiographical essays

Zagajewski remarks that his peregrinations instilled in him a particular mental filter, through which all geographical places seem equally dreamlike and phantasmagoric.

Zagajewski's generation, which also happens to be my generation, was the first to grow up in a world shaped entirely by the daily routines of "real socialism." Zagajewski's generation, which also happens to be my generation, was the first to grow up in a world shaped entirely by the daily routines of well-established "real socialism." The war, Stalinist terror, the frustrated hopes of 1956—years of conflict and trial—were the narrative of our parents' generation. Our own time in comparison seemed safe, undistinguished, static, offering very little choice about anything. For a young person trying to imagine his or her future, life looked like a deep well with diminishing, darkening rings of grimy concrete.

But in the late 1960s—the years of countercultural ferment in the West—our seemingly moribund history also started showing unexpected signs of life. Barely penetrable by the casual observer, there were factional struggles within the power elite and grumbling among disaffected intellectuals. What finally sparked the political upheaval was an appropriately Polish —that is, romantic and theatrical—event. In March of 1968, a Warsaw production of "The Forefathers' Eve," a venerated national drama by the nineteenth-century Polish poet Adam Mickiewicz, was closed down by the censor's office. The play's many anti-Russian allusions (it was written when Poland was jointly occupied by tsarist Russia, Prussia, and Austria) met with loud and unabashedly approving reactions from the Warsaw audience. After the production was canceled, a number of

prominent writers signed a protest letter, and students of Warsaw's many universities started demonstrating on their cam-
puses, just as if they lived in Paris or Berkeley.

The brutal reprisals by the authorities — beatings, vulgar in-
sults, arrests, and prison sentences — came as a total shock in-
dicative of the political innocence of our generation. When,
two years later, shipyard workers from Polish coastal towns
staged their own protest against food price increases and were
shot at and beaten by the security and military troops, previously isolated Polish dissident groups started to organize into
a clandestine opposition movement.

These were the formative experiences of a group of young
writers that came to be known as the New Wave or the Generation 68–70, to which Zagajewski belonged in the early years of
his career, together with his contemporaries Ewa Lipska, Stanislaw Baranczak, Ryszard Krynicki, Julian Kornhauser, and several others.

Despite the many poetic differences of these writers, there is
something unmistakably similar in their depictions of colorless
urban landscapes, pointless, repetitive activities, of sensually
and intellectually barren existence. Time and again, rebellion
and outrage seem to rise in their poems in a breathless crescendo to recede in helpless sarcasm and self-derision. One of
the favorite metaphors of this group, not unlike that in baroque
authors, is the human body or one of its organs — usually sick,
deformed, or in pain — struggling against encroaching decay.
Private and collective memories turn in obsessive nightmares,
and minds teeter on the brink of insanity. Neither God, nor art,
nor philosophical reflection seems to afford real consolation,

and occasional moments of dark humor only underscore the general sense of absurdity and futility.

Adam Zagajewski is the coauthor, with Kornhauser, of the group's manifesto, "The Unrepresented World." It calls for a literature focused on everyday experience and determined to unmask the moral, intellectual, and aesthetic squalor spawned (which was barely mentioned but clearly implied in the essay) by the odious political system. A good example of this poetic program is Zagajewski's poem "New World," written in the mid-1970s. Punctuated by an obsessive admonition, "don't be lulled," the poem takes the reader on a harrowing trip through the circles of painful memories, indefinite anxiety, repulsion, self-loathing, and grief.

Poets of the New Wave often had friends among the budding Polish opposition movement, and some of them, like Baranczak, combined literary work with social activism. In an interview conducted years later Zagajewski speaks about a "tremendous sense of liberation" when he signed one of the early protest letters circulated by the opposition.[2] He remembers it as an existential moment of self-definition that broke the "monotonous, flat rhythm of life." "Suddenly there were young, brave and intelligent people around me — people I would have no chance of encountering anywhere else. In our conversations there was almost something erotic, of course in a purely Platonic sense."

But just as the opposition was coming into its own, moving inevitably toward the fateful Solidarity revolution of 1980, Zagajewski was growing impatient with the cozy camaraderie and the general politicization of literature. Born of a protest against the generation's sense of entrapment, the discourse of the politico-literary dissident community itself started to look like a trap. It called for a new form of literary conformity, a forced adoption of a public role, answering constant calls to arms from one's comrades-in-battle.

Zagajewski voiced those doubts in his most important book of essays, *Solidarity, Solitude,* which is clearly a testimony of a personal crisis but also offers an insight into the dilemmas faced by the whole generation of Polish writers.[3] In many ways they resemble the dilemmas pondered much earlier by Witold Gombrowicz shortly after his self-chosen wartime exile to Argentina. What happens to a life built almost exclusively around a struggle with a political enemy? — Zagajewski asks. What happens to a writer who tries to participate in the collective life of his community? A cultural struggle against a collectivist political idea tends to impose its own brand of rigidity upon the literary imagination. "To be a Pole, to participate in the work of Polish literature, is practically the same as becoming a member of a religious order with very strict rules. . . . Anyone who has an idea offers it to the others, immediately wants to change it into law or obligation — as if fearing his own *tête-à-tête* with originality." In other words, when the cause seems so much greater than the individual, originality — a personal creative adventure — seems almost paramount to disloyalty.

What is more, observed Zagajewski, antitotalitarian literature conveniently defined evil as something coming always from the outside: from history, from the imposed ideology, from "inauthentic" social arrangements. This instilled in a writer a false sense of innocence: "Lo and behold, the miraculous and angelic cure, we became better than we really are, for all evil has been sucked out by the totalitarian beast. We became like angels." The angelic fallacy, in turn, subverts one of the writer's chief missions, which Zagajewski defines as "thinking against oneself" — and encouraging readers to think against themselves, too.

In addition, a lyrical rebellion against totalitarianism smacks of something over the top, even slightly ridiculous. The nobility of a spiritual mutiny, explained Zagajewski, stands in direct proportion to the nobility of the object of rebellion. Each true rebellion is a rebellion against a father, an act of defiance mixed with respect and love. Totalitarianism, says the poet, can never be a father — it is too base, simple, devoid of any claim to authority except brutal force: "It is not someone close to us who hides the key to our cell, only a cold and alien force, anonymous and slippery like a toad." Fighting a toad with poetry, suggests Zagajewski, is below poetry's dignity.

In *Solidarity, Solitude*, he proposes a radically different strategy: "We have to conquer totalitarianism in passing, on our way to greater things, in the direction of this or that reality, even though we may be unable to say exactly what reality is; in the direction of this or some other value, even though we might be conscious of the endless number of conflicts between the chosen values."

"On the way to greater things" well describes the phase in Zagajewski's career that started roughly with the publication in 1983 of the volume *Ode to Plurality*, which marked the beginning of his gradual abandonment of the poetics of public engagement, and reached its full expression in the next book of poetry,

To Go to Lvov, published in 1986.[4] In the most important poems in *To Go to Lvov* images of stifling confinement are replaced by motifs of a journey, discovery, rush of colors, endlessly changing landscapes suffused with unexpected radiance and clarity. Despair gives way to joy, curiosity, awe, and worshipful contemplation. Metaphysical and religious intimations, present already in Zagajewski's earlier poems, become bold and ecstatic.

If "The New World" was the summa of Zagajewski's New Wave idiom, this new sensibility finds its fullest expression in the volume's title poem, which celebrates the mythical, lost city of his birth. Built of short exclamations and rapidly changing images, the poem seems to rush forward propelled by a series of verbs denoting striving, escape, soaring, and emotional discharge. This rhapsodic form of the poem stands in peculiar contrast to its seemingly melancholy subject, which only occasionally is mentioned directly:

> I won't see you any more, so much death
> awaits you, why must every city
> become Jerusalem and every man a Jew

But the poem's coda comes as a burst of defiant laughter:

> it exists, quiet and pure as
> a peach. It is everywhere.

The loss of the real, tangible city seems to liberate its memory from the confines of time and makes it indestructible and eternal. Lvov, the city of family legends, is no more. It has blended with every city in the world — an invitation to a never-ending journey.

A similar attempt to escape the confines of "historical reality" is evident already in the earlier volume, especially in its title poem, "Ode to Plurality," which is a paean to the pure ecstasy of life, the abundance of ideas, "a wild run of poetry," "the shock of love," "the changing delight of seasons," "the pleasure of hearing" and "the pleasure of seeing," the inexhaustible memory of civilizations, and the "singular soul" that stands "before / this abundance. Two eyes, two hands, / ten inventive fingers, and / only one ego, the wedge of an orange, / the youngest of sisters."

The poems in those volumes, especially in *To Go to Lvov*, barely mention the events that must have absorbed every Pole at that time — the imposition of martial law, the crushing of the Solidarity movement, the apparent end of the dream of the poet's generation. Instead, one can hear a clear derision of those who believe the elemental life force can be plugged with a few tanks and squads of riot police.

Beginning with *Ode to Plurality*, each of Zagajewski's volumes contains several such rhapsodic, fast-moving poems — litanies of sounds, sights, seemingly disparate scenes — in which a child-like enchantment with life's sensual richness mixes with a longing to look beyond the horizon of ordinary human experience. No matter what their immediate subject, they always seem to marvel at the ocean of Being and at the human mind swimming freely in its ever-changing waters.

Sometimes the sense of "plurality" helps to reconcile the past with the present, as in "Elegy," in which, within thirty-five verses, the poet manages to reconstruct the whole monochrome, stillborn physical reality of communist life ("houses small / as Tartar ponies," "Soviet gods with swollen eyelids," "sour smell of gas, sweet smell of tedium") and its moral climate ("endless winters, / in which there dwelled, as if in ancient lindens, / sparrows and knives and friendship and leaves of treason"), and then bid it farewell with a firm, conciliatory handshake ("but we lived there, and not as strangers").

On occasion, the cavalcade slows down, and the worship of plurality is replaced with an intense experience of one particular moment that seems to expand into a small, self-contained universe. In the beautiful short poem "That's Sicily," the "three-cornered island" glimpsed during a night sea passage evokes in an instant of sensual delight ("the huge leaves / of hills swayed like a giant's dreams") the whole history of the world and a quiet contemplation of death. In "On Swimming," a lonely swimmer converses with the sea while

> Little village churches
> hold a fabric of silence so fine
> and old that even a breath
> could tear it.

Such moments of great clarity are in fact gentle religious epiphanies — the intensity of their delight seemingly contradicting their transitory, impermanent character. In "Moment" the poet reflects on one such experience:

> This moment, mortal as you or I,
> was full of boundless, senseless,
> silly joy, as if it knew
> something we didn't.

In many poems the poet's mind becomes a high-tuned, supersensitive receiver of ambiguous, sometimes unsettling, but always enchanting signals from a strange, almost animistic God, the master of contradictory elements, the source of both fervor and peace, overwhelming energy and meditative repose. Most often the poet perceives him as inhabiting simultaneously darkness and fire, as in "The Churches of France," which are "dark vessels, where the shy flame of a mighty light wanders," or in "The Dark God, The Light God," in which he seems to fluctuate between darkness and light, providing an "infinite background that imprisons / and pierces us." In the passionate prayer-poem "Tierra del Fuego" God resembles a Dionysian deity entreated to:

> open the boxes full of song,
> open the blood that pulses in aortas
> of animals and stones,
> light lanterns in black gardens.

Apart from such moments of sudden revelation, Zagajewski's God favors indirectness and disguise, as in "He Acts":

> He looks for the longest line,
> the road so circuitous
> it is barely visible, and fades away
> in suffering. Only blind men, only
> owls feel sometimes its dwindling trace
> under their eyelids.

On other occasions, God's presence is experienced as perfect absence, a sense of loneliness so absolute that it begets an indefinite presence to which the soul feels "linked painfully, gladly."

And sometimes he seems to personify the invisible architecture of the universe, a system of labyrinths and passages that inexplicably lead the wanderer from wisdom to uncertainty and from pain to joy ("The Gothic"). He can even be "the smallest poppy seed in the world, / bursting with greatness," "a spider web, the hiding place of the first cause, the proof of existence between blades of grass" ("A Fence, Chestnut Tree").

Most important, Zagajewski's God reconciles formlessness and form, thus making art possible. "I know that God would have to be both form and formlessness," says the author in *Solidarity, Solitude*. God the creator is like an artist, who knows that "form keeps chaos in a mortal embrace, all the muscles of form are painful — but joyous, too — tense, and because of this, yes, because of this, form feeds on chaos, grows on pieces of chaos, becomes stronger, more resilient, as if it had been vaccinated against deadly smallpox."

Occasionally the richness of Being in Zagajewski's poems becomes a thicket and God assumes the role of a trickster deliberately putting obstacles in the road by which a traveler tries to reach his light. In "The Three Kings," the Magi arrive hopelessly late for the epiphany, and one of them, like a tardy pupil, blurts out a litany of excuses: "Spring meadows detained us, cowslips, / the glances of country maidens." There is also a constant mixing of "grief, despair, delight and pride" in the endless transformations of things, as in "The Blackbird," in which the bird, clearly identified with the poet himself, sings "a gentle, jazzy tune" of farewell to a "funeral cortege" that appears "the same each evening, there, on the horizon's thread."

Quite often, those poems tell also about ecstasy's other side —

the sense of disappointment when the spark fails to light up or a pilgrimage must be suddenly aborted. A traveler in "September" is unable to find the house of the Czech poet Vladimir Holan, and the famous baroque churches of Prague appear to him as "deluxe health clubs for athletic saints." Mysterious voices that haunt the poet in "Out Walking" are drowned by the din of the city and never return. In poems like this, the mood often becomes dark and claustrophobic, oddly reminiscent of the atmosphere of Zagajewski's early, New Wave poems, only this time there is no "angelic cure" of totalitarianism to absorb the anger and save the soul from self-blame. Even in those poems, however, resounds a tone of expectation that seems to defy the onslaught of modern pessimism and resignation. Emptiness, meaninglessness, darkness are merely transitory subjective states, Zagajewski seems to admonish his readers, while that which is permanent and real is essentially good.

"New metaphysical poetry" is perhaps the best description of Zagajewski's project. Following in the footsteps of Czeslaw Milosz, he seems to search for a metaphysical vision fit for modern times, although in someone of his generation this search looks even more contrarian than in Milosz, raised as he was in the lingering premodern aura of his East European "native realm."

The term "metaphysical poetry" is famously ill defined. T. S. Eliot, writing on the English Metaphysical poets of the seventeenth century, saw the chief characteristic of metaphysical writing in the expressive unity of intellect and emotion, "a direct sensuous apprehension of thought, or a recreation of thought into feeling." He further described a metaphysical poet as some-one able to "devour" heterogeneous experience—mystical, sensual, intellectual, and emotive—and amalgamate it within highly complex poetic constructs. This kind of hunger is in fact one of Zagajewski's signature traits. So is the presence of a metaphysical dimension in the stricter, philosophical sense of looking beyond the confines of the physical reality. Whatever the poet happens to be writing about, we feel that he is con-stantly preoccupied with Being—not its particular parts—and tries to capture its perceived unity hidden under its apparent multiplicity.

In his long, autobiographical essay *Another Beauty*, Adam Zagajewski describes a personal, intimate experience that seems to have shaped his poetic sensibility.[5] He speaks about a sudden discovery that "there existed, right at hand, a rich, full wholeness of life, to which I belonged, along with others like me, a whole that I might someday grasp by way of thought or the written page, though I knew that I'd never get all of it." Elsewhere, he states that given enough patience and attentiveness "reality opens trustingly before us; we feel then that it is before us, whole."

In Zagajewski's view, the premonition of this wholeness and the confidence needed to try to reconstruct it out of images, notions, and syllables have almost completely vanished from contemporary, modern culture. In *Solidarity, Solitude*, he writes that we have succumbed to "negative spirituality" and claims that modern skepticism and ever-present irony extinguish "any kind of devotion, be it religious, patriotic, or even aesthetic, because it suspects subterfuge of pride, falsehood, vacuity—or perhaps our weakness — it sees a mask of deception everywhere, self-interest, the reflex of the heard, hypocrisy." Out of this suspicion, we surrender ourselves to the aesthetics of fragmentation and chaos, which drains energy from modern political, intellectual, and spiritual life.

Even in his New Wave period, Zagajewski spoke approvingly about those in his generation who rejected the anarchic, "carnivalesque" rebelliousness of Western counterculture and embraced directness, sincerity, and classical humanistic traditions. Later, in *Solidarity, Solitude,* he claimed that "it is almost certain that Solidarity could not have arisen in an aura of anarchic culture" and praised the aesthetic choices made by the majority of independent Polish artists and intellectuals: "Building a cultural sensitivity on an 'axis of order' — to put it like a structuralist — was a coup in Polish intellectual life and it had almost immediate repercussions in the political sphere. Intellectual life became more serious, closer to metaphysical issues both in classically Christian and somewhat heretical senses. The internal tension, the pressure of spiritual life, grew."

Zagajewski believes that the radical skepticism and pervasive irony of modern art made it sterile, deprived of the spirit of adventure and discovery. Modern culture suffers from self-induced myopia and has all but abolished all pursuit of greatness. In *Another Beauty* he calls for the rectification of what he sees as a hopelessly one-sided, depressingly monochrome view of reality in contemporary literature and art: "There are two attitudes that you can take to the world. You can side with the tight-lipped skeptics and cynics who gleefully belittle life's phenomena, reducing them to a series of minute, self-evident, even commonplace components. Or, option two, you can accept the possibility that great unseen things do exist and, without resorting to lofty rhetoric or [the] intolerable bombast of itinerant Bible-thumpers, you can try to express them, or at least pay them tribute."

In 1999 Zagajewski published what is probably his most impassioned and personal manifesto, "The Shabby and the Sublime," in which he accused much "writing and thinking in recent years" of being "meager, gray, thin, anemic," a mere "chatter of self-satisfied craftsmen."[6] The reason for this sorry state of literature (Zagajewski later narrows his argument to poetry) is what he calls "an anti-metaphysical program" of deliberate exclusion from the poet's sphere of interest of anything that reaches beyond the everyday and the ordinary — that touches on greatness, heroism, sainthood, the higher aspiration of the human spirit. Contemporary writing, argues Zagajewski, suffers from pathological aversion to the sublime, which, after the classical author known as Longinus, he describes as "a spark that leaps from the soul of the writer to the soul of his reader and the mysterious echo of a noble spirit." Only a few moderns managed to resist this tendency, Zagajewski says. His list is as short as it is illustrious: Friedrich Hoelderlin, W. B. Yeats, Rainer Maria Rilke, Osip Mandelstam, the Polish post-Romantic poet-thinker Cyprian Norwid, and, of course, Milosz (but no Eliot!). "There really is a higher voice that sometimes speaks," but most of modern poetry chooses not to hear it, he insists.

But Zagajewski is also aware of the dangers awaiting anybody who challenges the skeptical, down-to-earth spirit of modern culture. The most serious, perhaps, is the temptation of faux innocence, the nostalgic allure of a seemingly idyllic premodern past. In "The Shabby and the Sublime" he writes that those searching for a "metaphysical shudder" would be wise to avoid the poetic "neoclassical pomp, its Alpine stage-set excess, its theatrical overkill." Zagajewski calls for a new concept of "high style" suitable for loftier, grander subject matter but warns against sententiousness and a preacherly tone. The writer, says Zagajewski, must not cease to be "everyman," to carefully mediate between the world of the spirit and the world of seemingly trivial affairs of contemporary life.

Does Zagajewski the Metaphysical poet achieve what he calls for in his essays? and does he avoid the dangers of the metaphysical project?

Despite his praise of the high style, his own poetic diction is usually simple and direct, only slightly elevated — through rhythms and sonorities — above everyday, conversational speech. It is a perfectly modulated, controlled "medium style," typical of much of the Polish postwar poetry of Milosz, Zbigniew Herbert, and Wislawa Szymborska (in her more "classicist" and meditative poems). In many of his poems, sufficiently many to count him among the great poetic voices of his generation, Zagajewski can fill this style with remarkable energy and originality. And yet, in many others he seems unable to resist the allure of such slushy tropes as "a mountain stream scented with willows," "dew on the grass," "a nightingale among the branches." In one poem ("Anecdote of Rain") the author gives us "tents of trees," "raindrops," "soft air," "wet leaves," not to mention suffering, sobbing, the scent of spring, and the scent of sorrow — all within eight short lines.

It is also a bit disconcerting that Zagajewski's epiphanies seem to require a degree of background elegance and refinement, preferably Italian hill-towns and Mediterranean islands, interiors of Gothic churches, and bucolic landscapes. Transcendental experiences happen mostly in the presence of masterpieces or glorious natural vistas. It may appear that Zagajewski's God would have little to say to someone who has never drunk the honey warmth of Tuscany, been pierced to the core by a Beethoven quartet, or bathed in the light of a Vermeer. Zagajewski's metaphysical excitements sometimes come uncomfortably close to dandyish aestheticism, the turn-of-the-century religion of Beauty, which was denounced, among others, by Milosz. It is also hard to ignore the literary, not to say bookish, provenience of many of his metaphors, which makes them sound, to quote Samuel Johnson's judgment on the original Metaphysical poets, like "descriptions copied from descriptions, imitations borrowed from imitations."

What is more, Zagajewski's lyrical persona is certainly no "everyman." Instead, we encounter, time and again, a self-regarding aristocrat of the spirit, a connoisseur of higher experiences, a consciousness floating a notch above the rest of us. Unlike Walt Whitman, who wanted to identify with millions, Zagajewski's *porte-parole* most of the time walks alone. Sometimes we glimpse the presence of a lover, a companion in ecstasy. Only rarely, as in the poem "The Greenhouse," "other people's doors swing open for a moment, / you read their hidden thoughts, their holidays don't hurt, / their happiness is less opaque, their faces / almost beautiful." More often, however, the "other people" come into focus as an annoyance or an object of condescending pity. In "Senza Flash," an aesthetic moment in a museum is spoiled by "tourists smiling in their spotless shirts," "slow and steady, docile, drowsy, / hands stained black from daily papers, / faces thick with cream." In "Europe in Winter," "the holiday hordes, possessed / by one urge only, the urge for yellow gold, / throng the broad, damp boulevards, / and your museums are shut down by strikes." In "Square d'Orleans," the poet is disconcerted by the fact that the district of Paris where Frédéric Chopin once lived has become a business hub where "dapper gentlemen enter and exit, / each slim as a new banknote" and "insurance agents flourish, and the doctor / receives his patients at appointed hours." What if the businesslike crowd contains another sublime soul, perhaps one of the insurance agents, who secretly adores Chopin's music? Thoughts like that rarely invade the comfortable space between the poet and his fellow men: he — the pilgrim; we — tourists, passersby, commuters.

When the illumination refuses to come or when ecstasy is suddenly extinguished, our hero's aristocratic aloofness turns into aristocratic spleen that no common pleasure or human companionship is able to alleviate. In this state, which is the subject of many of Zagajewski's poems, "common" people become unwelcome visitors from everyday life who try to bring the poet down to their own level. But if a sudden, rare shock of inspiration is the only thing worth living for, then the existence of much of humanity is quite pointless and inconsequential. Is this the subliminal message beyond Zagajewski's meta-physical vision?

"I doubt one can express 'everything.' To express 'every-thing' is not the task of just one author, perhaps it is the uto-pian goal of mankind. But to hear everything, just as one hears a mountain cascade — to hear the sound of everything — this seems indispensable, life giving," writes Zagajewski in *Solidar-ity, Solitude.* But with the exception of his best poems, like "To Go to Lvov," his poetic hearing is oddly selective. Rather than a Metaphysical poet in touch with "wholeness," he resembles a Romantic outcast — detached, proud, and a bit surly.

In fact, the "amalgamation" of thought and feeling that Eliot wrote about is a rare occurrence in Zagajewski's poetry. When Eliot, in "Little Gidding," tells about the midwinter journey, when "between melting and freezing / the soul's sap quivers," even a profoundly skeptical reader feels that something strange and wondrous is happening to the poem's narrator on that par-ticular night. Moments like this do happen in Zagajewski's verse, but too frequently he seems to doubt the strength of his metaphor and follows it with a wordy explication: "We've been locked in the world's box, / love sets us free, time kills us"; "We live in longing. In our dreams, / locks and bolts open up"; "Poetry calls us to a higher life, / but what's low is just as eloquent." To borrow another of Eliot's distinctions, Zaga-jewski is only rarely an "intellectual poet." For the most part he is a "poet that ruminates."

Those ruminations often lead to some truly interesting intel-lectual questions, but the author rarely makes the effort to ad-dress them squarely. There is, for example, the perplexing (and truly metaphysical) problem of evil—its origin, its manifestations, and its multiple effects on the human mind. The poet admits that not all the monsters that inhabit modern consciousness are fabrications of modern "negative spirituality." Some of them may even be real and much older than modernity. But in his crusade against negativism, Zagajewski seems too eager to push them to the periphery of his vision to make room for what he sees as an all-encompassing goodness of being: "Above all, though, I detect the exceptionally patient and persistent work of goodness, which could not be completely extinguished even in this rather cruel century," he writes in *Another Beauty*. "Goodness does exist! Not just evil, stupidity, and Satan. Evil has more energy and can act with the speed of lightning, like a blitzkrieg, whereas goodness likes to dawdle in the most peculiar fashion."

There is little doubt that goodness does exist, and one should certainly hope it will never be extinguished. But unfortunately, in our daily life we deal not with abstract Goodness or Evil but with very concrete results of evil acts. It is they that we are expected to address, remedy, or overcome. Even a poet cannot eschew that dilemma. Zagajewski believes that in our "negativist" times poetry's function is to praise. "But why write poems that are only a lament, a repetition of our nightmares?" he said in an interview.[7] "I see no reason to howl. Writing is an experience of another order of the world, and it exists only for a fraction of a second. Without such illuminations there would be no poetry of any kind. Even the darkest poems need illumination."

But illumination should not blind. Finding illumination while at the same time acknowledging the darkness in which we so often dwell is a problem that Zagajewski seems unable to resolve — either philosophically or lyrically. He rhetorically admits the existence of evil, but his admissions have a peculiarly abstract and offhand quality, while the ease with which he proceeds to comfort our souls is more than a bit uncomfortable. When the interviewer criticized Zagajewski for "silencing the drama of the world," the poet answered by pointing to the poems "Lava" or "Watching *Shoah*." "My ideal," he says, "is a clash of suffering with a more peaceful aesthetic realm, . . . a confrontation between beauty and suffering," which are like "brothers." But in Zagajewski's poetry this confrontation takes the form of a meditative juxtaposition rather than a clash of opposite elements. Whenever pain and beauty meet, the poet attempts to negotiate a "peaceful solution" between them by arguing that the summa of the opposites is always more beautiful than painful. In "Watching *Shoah* in a Hotel Room in America," gruesome images of the Holocaust (wagons of human hair, pyramids of shoes in Auschwitz) contrast with the peaceful, almost somnolent tone of the poem, with death dissolving slowly into silence and sleep. "Lava" seems to suggest that a plus and a minus of the same value must give a positive number rather than a zero:

> Lava kills and preserves, the heart beats
> and is beaten; there was war then there wasn't;
> Jews died, Jews stayed alive, cities are razed,
> cities endure, love fades, the kiss everlasting,
> the wings of the hawk must be brown,
> you're still with me though we're no more,
> ships sink, sand sings, clouds wander
> like wedding veils in tatters.

The poem ends with the return of dawn "hoary with dew."

While ecstasy in Zagajewski's poetry is usually personal and directly experienced, evil is observed from a certain abstracting distance that seems to deprive it of its mind-shattering power. One of the most striking examples of this is "Try To Praise the Mutilated World," which has been read as a response to the attacks of September 11, 2001. The sum total of pain in the world is dealt with in a handful of fleeting images of "refugees going nowhere," "abandoned homesteads of exiles," the "salty oblivion" awaiting ships that will never reach their destination, unspecified "earth's scars." Pain and desolation seem to be located mainly in the past, perceived in already fading aftermaths of tragedies. We are spared any glimpse of whatever has caused the "earth's scars," or what was done to the people that once inhabited the "abandoned homesteads." Let us not dwell on these things too long, the author seems to suggest. Let's focus on the world's many glories and sensual delights, depicted in the poem in much more immediate and dynamic language: "June's long days, / and wild strawberries, drops of wine, the dew," moments spent with someone dear in a white room with a fluttering curtain, music, "acorns in the park in autumn," a bird's gray feather, and "the gentle light that strays and vanishes, / and returns." The poem is often quoted as a token of Zagajewski's mature, clear-eyed humanism, yet it begs the question whether long June days and the taste of strawberries provide a sufficient counterweight to genocide. It may, indeed, be imperative to praise this mutilated (and mutilating) world, but at this late time in history, we may need a better reason than this world's occasional delightfulness. If the blood-drenched world can also be experienced as wondrous and worth continuing, it is probably through a challenge it poses to the moral mind, and not through its soft breezes and fragrant smells. But Zagajewski's mind — at least the mind expressed in his poetry — seems too much at rest for such an engagement. He opens his poetic lens and applies a series of well-chosen filters until the right image appears in view. He says he wants to behold everything, but then he gently averts his eyes.

There is little doubt that Adam Zagajewski is one of the most original poetic voices of his generation, and the surprising weaknesses of his poetry may in fact be the side effect of his strength and originality. His lucid, inventive language and his sharp, analytical intelligence seem strangely at odds with his programmatic goal of rejecting modern self-doubt and irony. Sometimes, in his essays more often than in his verse, he seems to realize that something in his approach has not been properly resolved. In one of his more recent essays, "Against Poetry," which treats the nature of poetic "ecstasy," we find this striking confession: "But we can't know if our enthusiasm actually corresponds to anything in reality, in the world's structure, even though in moments of exaltation we're absolutely convinced this is so, and even the next day we're still sure we're right. In a week or two, though, doubts may begin to appear."[8] One would wish that this sort of reservation were part of the fabric of his own poetry. It could save his quite real poetic ardor from the artificialities of high style and disrobe it of the literary costumes in which it tends to clothe itself.

Finally, it is perhaps the bold metaphysical aspiration that weighs most heavily on Zagajewski's poetry. In another essay from *A Defense of Ardor* ("Nietzsche in Krakow") he claims that poetry may lead the reader to an appreciation of wholeness through "suggestions, allusions, a net full of metaphors," rather than through "one central metaphor." This is undoubtedly true. But in true metaphysical poetry those suggestions and allusions are held together by one central metaphysical Idea. For the Metaphysical poets of the seventeenth century it was the Christian concept of infinite love among infinite suffering. Modern metaphysical poets like Milosz and Eliot were searching for such an Idea, and that search informed their poetry with intellectual and expressive unity. In the case of Zagajewski, however, despite his many religious references, this idea seems merely a postulate, a wish, a vacant space surrounded by "a net full of metaphors." This creates a fissure at the very heart of Zagajewski's world, something that asks to be acknowledged, studied, made part of the poetic project. Unfortunately, Zagajewski makes it into the stuff of poetic decorum.

In the end, we wish he would more often leave himself more breathing space, look from a distance on his poetic persona, listen to the world, contemplate his "double-headed doubt," and occasionally even mock its own lofty dreams, as in the poem "Cicadas," in which the poet seems to admit that to reconcile daily tedium with flashes of ecstasy, pain with delight into one divine whole may be one of the soul's grand unachievable desires: "We exist between the elements, / between fire and sleep. / Pain chases / or outstrips us."

NOTES

Bruno Schulz: The Prisoner of Myth

1. Jerzy Ficowski, *Regions of the Great Heresy: Bruno Schulz, A Biographical Portrait*, trans. Theodosia Robertson (New York: W. W. Norton, 2003).

2. Jerzy Ficowski, *A Reading of Ashes*, trans. Keith Bosley and Krystyna Wandycz (Lowicz: Browarna, 1993). Jerzy Ficowski is also one of few translators of Yiddish and Roma poetry into Polish. For Ficowski's poetry in Polish, see *Poezje wybrane* (Warsaw: Ludowa Spoldzielnia Wydawnicza, 1982) and *Wszystko czego nie wiem* (Sejny: Pogranicze, 1999).

3. Jerzy Ficowski, *Regiony wielkiej herezji* (Krakow: Wydawnictwo Literackie, 1967).

4. Jerzy Ficowski, ed., *Ksiega listow/Bruno Schulz* (Krakow: Wydawnictwo Literackie, 1975).

5. The letters by Schulz cited in this chapter come from the selection in *The Regions of the Great Heresy*.

6. Henryk Grynberg, *Drohobycz, Drohobycz and Other Stories: True Tales from the Holocaust and Life After*, trans. Alicia Nitecki, ed. Theodosia Robertson (New York: Penguin, 2002).

7. For a representative sample of Schulz's art, see Jerzy Ficowski, ed., *The Drawings of Bruno Schulz* (Evanston: Northwestern University Press, 1990).

8. Editions of Schulz's prose works cited in this chapter are *Sanatorium Under the Sign of the Hourglass*, trans. Celina Wieniewska

183

(Boston: Houghton Mifflin, 1977), and *The Street of Crocodiles*, trans. Celina Wieniewska (New York: Penguin, 1977). Also see *Collected Works of Bruno Schulz*, ed. Jerzy Ficowski (London: Picador, 1998).

9. Rainer Maria Rilke, *Ahead of All Parting: The Selected Poetry and Prose of Rainer Maria Rilke*, ed. and trans. Stephen Mitchell (New York: Modern Library, 1995).

Witold Gombrowicz: The Transforming Self

1. Witold Gombrowicz, *Diary*, trans. Lillian Vallee, 3 vols. (Evanston: Northwestern University Press, 1988–93). Unless otherwise specified, the notes refer to the most recent English-language editions.

2. Witold Gombrowicz, *A Kind of Testament*, ed. Dominique de Roux, trans. Alastair Hamilton (Philadelphia: Temple University Press, 1973).

3. Witold Gombrowicz, *Bacacay*, trans. Bill Johnston (New York: Archipelago Books, 2004); Witold Gombrowicz, *Ferdydurke*, trans. Danuta Borchardt (New Haven: Yale University Press, 2000).

4. Witold Gombrowicz, *Pornografia*, trans. Alastair Hamilton (New York: Grove Press, 1967).

5. Witold Gombrowicz, *Cosmos*, trans. Danuta Borchardt (New Haven: Yale University Press, 2005).

6. Witold Gombrowicz, *The Marriage*, trans. Louis Iribarne (New York: Grove Press, 1969); Witold Gombrowicz, *Ivona, Princess of Burgundia*, trans. Krystyna Griffith-Jones and Catherine Robins (New York: Grove Press, 1970).

7. Witold Gombrowicz, *Operetta*, trans. Louis Iribarne (London: Calder and Boyars, 1971).

Stanislaw Ignacy Witkiewicz: Modernism to Madness

1. Stanislaw Ignacy Witkiewicz, *Insatiability: A Novel*, trans., in a newly revised version, Louis Iribarne (Evanston: Northwestern University Press, 1996).
2. For a discussion of Witkiewicz's graphic art, see Irena Jakimowicz, *Witkacy the Painter*, trans. Ewa Krasinska (Warsaw: Auriga, 1987).
3. Quoted from *The Witkiewicz Reader*, ed., trans., and introd. Daniel Gerould (Evanston: Northwestern University Press, 1992).
4. A prolific translator of Witkiewicz's dramas, Daniel Gerould is also the author of, among other critical works, *Witkacy: A Study of Stanislaw Ignacy Witkiewicz as an Imaginative Writer* (Seattle: University of Washington Press, 1981).
5. *622 upadki Bunga czyli demoniczna kobieta*, partial translation in *The Witkiewicz Reader; Jedyne wyjscie*, no English translation; *Pozegnanie jesieni*, partial translation in *The Witkiewicz Reader*.
6. For the first attempt, see *Insatiability: A Novel in Two Parts*, trans. with introd. and commentary Louis Iribarne (Urbana: University of Illinois Press, 1977).

Czeslaw Milosz: A Testament of Exile

1. *Legends of Modernity: Essays and Letters from Occupied Poland, 1942–43*, trans. Madeleine G. Levine (New York: Farrar, Straus and Giroux, 2005).
2. Milosz's poetry quoted from *New and Collected Poems 1931–2001* (New York: Ecco, 2001).
3. *The Captive Mind*, trans. Jane Zielonko (New York: Knopf, 1953).
4. *The Land of Ulro*, trans. Louis Iribarne (New York: Farrar, Straus and Giroux, 1984).
5. *Road-Side Dog*, trans. Czeslaw Milosz and Robert Hass (New York: Farrar, Straus and Giroux, 1998).

6. *Native Realm: A Search for Self-Definition*, trans. Catherine S. Leach (Garden City: Doubleday, 1968).

Zbigniew Herbert: The Darkness of Mr. Cogito

1. Zbigniew Herbert, *89 wierszy* (Krakow: "a5," 1998).
2. Unless otherwise indicated, all English quotations from Herbert's poetry are from Zbigniew Herbert, *The Collected Poems, 1956–1998*, trans. and ed. Alissa Valles, with additional translations by Czeslaw Milosz and Peter Dale Scott (New York: Ecco, 2007). The vast majority of the poems in that volume were translated by Alissa Valles, and the translations in my text, unless otherwise noted, are by her. Those translated by Czeslaw Milosz and Peter Dale Scott are identified on first mention by "M/S."
3. *Barbarian in the Garden*, trans. Michael March and Jaroslaw Anders (Manchester: Carcanet, 1985). First Polish edition: 1965; *Still Life with a Bridle*, trans. John and Bogdana Carpenter (New York: Ecco, 1991); *The Labyrinth on the Sea*, trans. John Carpenter and Bogdana Carpenter (New York: Ecco, 2005).
4. My translation.
5. D. J. Enright, *The Alluring Problem: An Essay on Irony* (Oxford: Oxford University Press, 1986).
6. In *Renaissance and Modern Studies* 6 (1962).
7. *Selected Poems*, trans. Czeslaw Milosz and Peter Dale Scott (Harmondsworth: Penguin Books, 1968).
8. *The King of the Ants*, trans. John and Bogdana Carpenter (New York: Ecco, 1999).
9. My translations.
10. A. Alvarez, "Noble Poet," *New York Review of Books*, July 18, 1985.

Wislawa Szymborska: The Power of Preserving

1. Unless otherwise specified, quoted after Wislawa Szymborska, *Poems, New and Collected, 1957–1997*, trans. Stanislaw Baranczak and Clare Cavanagh (New York: Harcourt Brace, 1998).
2. Translations marked (JT) are quoted from Wislawa Szymborska, *Miracle Fair: Selected Poems by Wislawa Szymborska*, trans. Joanna Trzeciak (New York: W. W. Norton, 2001). This slender volume includes ten highly elliptical poems that Baranczak and Cavanagh, citing "unsurmountable problems of a technical nature," omitted from their otherwise inspired collection.

Gustaw Herling-Grudzinski: Sleepless in Naples

1. Gustaw Herling-Grudzinski, *A World Apart* (London: Heinemann, 1951).
2. Excerpts from this six-volume work were published in English as *Volcano and Miracle: A Selection of Fiction and Nonfiction from The Journal Written at Night*, trans. Ronald Strom (New York: Viking, 1996).
3. *The Island: Three Tales*, trans. Ronald Strom (New York: Viking, 1993).
4. *The Noonday Cemetery and Other Stories*, trans. Bill Johnson (New York: New Directions, 2003).

Tadeusz Konwicki: Polish Endgame

1. *Wladza* (Warsaw: Czytelnik, 1954).
2. English edition: *A Dreambook for Our Time*, trans. David Welsh (Cambridge: MIT Press, 1969).
3. *Zwierzoczlekoupior* (Warsaw: Czytelnik, 1969), English edition, *The Anthropos-Spectre-Beast*, trans. George and Audrey Korwin-Rodziszewski (New York: S. Phillips, 1977); *Wniebowstapienie* (Warsaw: Iskry, 1967).

4. *Kompleks Polski* (Warsaw: NOWA, 1977), English edition, *The Polish Complex*, trans. Richard Lourie (New York: Farrar, Straus and Giroux, 1982); *Mala apokalipsa* (Warsaw: NOWA, 1979), English edition, *A Minor Apocalypse*, trans. Richard Lourie (New York: Farrar, Straus and Giroux, 1983).

Adam Zagajewski: To Hear the Sound of Everything

1. *Mysticism for Beginners*, trans. Clare Cavanagh (New York: Farrar, Straus and Giroux, 1997). Poems from this volume were later included in Adam Zagajewski, *Without End: New and Selected Poems*, trans. Clare Cavanagh, Renata Gorczynski, Benjamin Ivry, and C. K. Williams (New York: Farrar, Straus and Giroux, 2002). Unless otherwise indicated, quotations from Adam Zagajewski's poetry are from this volume, which is the most complete presentation of Zagajewski's poetry in English.
2. In Stanislaw Beres, *Historia literatury polskiej w rozmowach* (Warsaw: W.A.B., 2002). Quotes are my translations.
3. *Solidarity, Solitude: Essays*, trans. Lillian Vallee (New York: Ecco, 1990), first published in Polish as *Solidarnosc i samotnosc* (Paris: Cahiers Litteraires, 1986).
4. *Jechac do Lwowa i inne wiersze* (Krakow: Margines, 1986, and Warsaw: Droga, 1986).
5. *Another Beauty*, trans. Clare Cavanagh (Athens: University of Georgia Press, 2002).
6. In *A Defense of Ardor*, trans. Clare Cavanagh (New York: Farrar, Straus and Giroux, 2004).
7. In *Historia literatury*. My translation.
8. In *A Defense of Ardor*.

SUGGESTED READING

Contemporary Polish Literature

Kridl, Manfred. *A Survey of Polish Literature and Culture.* Translated by Olga Scherer-Virsky. New York: Columbia University Press, 1956.

Krzyzanowski, Julian. *A History of Polish Literature.* Translated by Doris Ronowicz. Warsaw: PWN, 1978.

Milosz, Czeslaw. *The History of Polish Literature.* Berkeley: University of California Press, 1983.

Peterkiewicz, Jerzy. *Polish Literature from the European Perspective: Studies and Treaties.* Lodz: Lodzkie Towarzystwo Nauk, 2006.

Ten Centuries of Polish Literature. Translated by Daniel Sax. Warsaw: PAN, 2004.

Bruno Schulz

Banner, Gillian. *Holocaust Literature: Schulz, Levi, Spiegelman and Memory of the Offence.* London: Vallentine Mitchell, 2000.

Brown, Russel E. *Myths and Relatives: Seven Essays on Bruno Schulz.* Muenchen: Verlag Otto Sanger, 1991.

Ficowski, Jerzy. *Regions of the Great Heresy: Bruno Schulz, a Portrait.* Edited and translated by Theodosia Robertson. New York: W. W. Norton, 2003.

Prokopczyk, Czeslaw Z. *Bruno Schulz: New Documents and Interpretations.* New York: Peter Lang, 1999.

Schulz, Bruno. *The Book of Idolatory*. Edited by Jerzy Ficowski. Translated by Bogna Piotrowska. Warsaw: Interpress, [1988?].

———. *Collected Works of Bruno Schulz*. Edited by Jerzy Ficowski. London: Picador, 1998.

———. *The Complete Fiction of Bruno Schulz*. Translated by Celina Wieniewska. New York: Walker, 1989.

———. *The Drawings of Bruno Schulz*. Edited by Jerzy Ficowski. Evanston: Northwestern University Press, 1990.

———. Drawings of Bruno Schulz: From the Collection of the Adam Mickiewicz Museum of Literature, Warsaw. Jerusalem: Israel Museum, 1990.

———. *Letters and Drawings of Bruno Schulz: With Selected Prose*. Edited by Jerzy Ficowski. Translated by Walter Arnd and Victoria Nelson. New York: Harper and Row, c.1988.

———. *Sanatorium Under the Sign of the Hourglass*. Translated by Celina Wieniewska. New York: Penguin Books, 1979.

———. *The Street of Crocodiles*. Translated by Celina Wieniewska. New York: Walker [1963].

———. *The Street of Crocodiles*. Translated by Michael Kandel. c.1963. Reprint New York: Penguin Books, 1977.

Stala, Krzysztof. *On the Margins of Reality: The Paradoxes of Representation in Bruno Schulz's Fiction*. Stockholm: Almqvist and Wiksell International, 1993.

Witold Gombrowicz

Gombrowicz, Witold. *A Guide to Philosophy in Six Hours and Fifteen Minutes*. Translated by Benjamin Ivry. New Haven: Yale University Press, 2004.

———. *Bacacay*. Translated by Bill Johnston. New York: Archipelago Books, 2004.

———. *Cosmos*. English version by Eric Mosbacher. London: Mac-Gibbon and Kee, 1967.

———. *Cosmos*. Translated by Danuta Borchardt. New Haven: Yale University Press, 2005.

———. *Diary*. Edited by Jan Kot. Translated by Lillian Vallee. 3 vols. Evanston: Northwestern University Press, 1988–93.

———. *Ferdydurke*. Translated by Eric Mosbacher. New York: Marion Boyars, 2005.

———. *Ferdydurke*. Translated by Danuta Borchardt. New Haven: Yale University Press, 2000.

———. *Ivona, Princess of Burgundia*. Translated by Krystyna Griffith-Jones and Catherine Robins. New York: Grove Press, [1970, 1969].

———. *A Kind of Testament*. Edited by Dominique de Roux. Translated by Alastair Hamilton. Champaign: Dalkey Archive Press, 2007.

———. *The Marriage*. Translated by Louis Iribarne. New York: Grove Press, [c.1969].

———. *Polish Memories*. Translated by Bill Johnston. New Haven: Yale University Press, 2004.

———. *Pornografia*. Translated from the French by Alaister Hamilton. New York: Grove Press, [1967, c.1966].

———. *Possessed, or the Secret of Myslotch: A Gothic Novel*. English version by J. A. Underwood. London, New York: M. Boyars, 1988.

———. *Trans-Atlantyk*. Translated by Carolyn French and Nina Karsov. New Haven: Yale University Press, 1994.

Kuczaba, Alex. *Gombrowicz and Frish: Aspects of the Literary Diary*. Bonn: Bouvier, 1980.

Thompson, Ewa M. *Witold Gombrowicz*. Boston: Twayne Publishers, 1979.

Stanislaw Ignacy Witkiewicz (Witkacy)

Gerould, Daniel. *Witkacy: Stanislaw Ignacy Witkiewicz as an Imaginative Writer*. Seattle: University of Washington Press, 1981.

Jakimowicz, Irena. *Witkacy, the Painter*. Translated by Ewa Krasinska. Warsaw: Auriga, 1985.

Twentieth-Century Polish Avant-Garde Drama: Plays, Scenarios, Critical Documents. Translated by Daniel Gerould. Ithaca: Cornell University Press, 1977.

Witkiewicz, Stanislaw Ignacy. *Country House.* Translated by Daniel Gerould. Amsterdam: Harwood Academic Publishers, 1997.

———. *Insatiability: A Novel in Two Parts.* Translated by Louis Iribarne. Urbana: University of Illinois Press, 1977.

———. *Insatiability: A Novel.* Translated by Louis Iribarne. Evanston: Northwestern University Press, 1996.

———. *The Madman and the Nun & The Crazy Locomotive: Three Plays, Including "The Water Hen."* Translated by Daniel Gerould and C. S. Durer. New York: Applause Theatre Book Publishers, 1988.

———. *The Mother and Other Unsavory Plays: Including The Shoemakers and They.* Translated by Daniel Gerould and C. S. Durer. New York: Applause Theatre Book Publishers, 1993.

———. "The New Deliverance." Translated by Adam Tungu, *Polish Perspectives,* no. 6 (1963).

———. *Seven Plays.* Translated by Daniel Gerould. New York: Martin E. Segal Theatre Centre Publications, 2004.

———. *Tropical Madness: Four Plays.* Translated by Daniel Gerould and Eleanor Gerould. New York: Winter House, 1972.

———. *The Witkiewicz Reader.* Edited by Daniel Gerould. Evanston: Northwestern University Press, 1992.

Czeslaw Milosz

Czarnecka, Ewa, and Aleksander Fiut. *Conversations With Czeslaw Milosz.* Translated by Richard Lourie. San Diego: Harcourt, 1987.

Davie, Donald. *Czeslaw Milosz and the Insufficiency of Lyric.* Knoxville: University of Tennessee Press, 1986.

Fiut, Aleksander. *The Eternal Moment: The Poetry of Czeslaw Milosz.* Translated by Theodosia S. Robertson. Berkeley: University of California Press, 1990.

Milosz, Czeslaw. *Beginning With My Streets: Essays and Recollections*. New York: Farrar, Straus and Giroux, 1991.

———. *To Begin Where I Am: Selected Essays*. Edited by Bogdana Carpenter and Madeline G. Levine. New York: Farrar, Straus and Giroux, 2001.

———. *Bells in Winter*. Translated by Lillian Vallee. New York: Ecco Press, 1978.

———. *A Book of Luminous Things*. Edited by Czeslaw Milosz. New York: Harcourt, 1996.

———. *The Captive Mind*. Translated by Jane Zielonko. c.1953. Reprint New York: Octagon Books, 1981.

———. *The Collected Poems, 1931–1987*. New York: Ecco Press, 1988.

———. *Emperor of the Earth: Modes of Eccentric Vision*. Berkeley: University of California Press, 1977.

———. *Facing the River*. Translated by the author and Robert Hass. Hopewell: Ecco Press, 1995.

———. *The Issa Valley*. Translated by Louis Iribarne. New York: Farrar, Straus and Giroux, 1981.

———. *The Land of Ulro*. Translated by Louis Iribarne. New York: Farrar, Straus and Giroux, 1984.

———. *Legends of Modernity: Essays and Letters from Poland, 1942–43*. Translated by Madeleine G. Levine. New York: Farrar, Straus and Giroux, 2005.

———. *Milosz's ABC's*. Translated by Madeline G. Levine. New York: Farrar, Straus and Giroux, 2001.

———. *Native Realm: A Search for Self-Definition*. Translated by Catherine S. Leach. New York: Farrar, Straus and Giroux, 2002.

———. *New and Collected Poems 1931–2001*. New York: Ecco Press, 2001.

———. *Nobel Lecture*. New York: Farrar, Straus and Giroux, 1980.

———. *Provinces*. Translated by the author and Robert Hass. New York: Ecco Press, 1991.

——. *Road-Side Dog*. Translated by the author and Robert Hass. New York: Farrar, Straus and Giroux, 1998.

——. *Second Space: New Poems*. Translated by the author and Robert Hass. New York: Ecco Press, 2004.

——. *The Seizure of Power*. Translated by Celina Wieniewska. New York: Farrar, Straus and Giroux, 1982.

——. *Selected Poems*. c.1973. Reprint New York: Ecco Press, 1980.

——. *Selected Poems, 1931–2004*. New York: HarperCollins, 2006.

——. *The Separate Notebook*. Translated by Robert Hass and Robert Pinsky with the author and Renata Gorczynski. New York: Ecco Press, 1984.

——. *Striving Towards Being: The Letters of Thomas Merton and Czeslaw Milosz*. Edited by Robert Faggen. New York: Farrar, Straus and Giroux, 1997.

——. *A Treatise on Poetry*. Translated by the author and Robert Hass. New York: Ecco Press, 2001.

——. *Visions from San Francisco Bay*. Translated by Richard Lourie. New York: Farrar, Straus and Giroux, 1982.

——. *The Witness of Poetry*. Cambridge: Harvard University Press, 1983.

——. *The World: Twenty Poems in Polish*. Translated by Czeslaw Milosz. San Francisco: Arion Press, 1989.

——. *A Year of the Hunter*. Translated by Madeline G. Levine. New York: Farrar, Straus and Giroux, 1994.

Volynska-Bogert, Rimma. *Czeslaw Milosz, An International Bibliography*. Ann Arbor: Dept. of Slavic Languages and University of Michigan, 1983.

Zbigniew Herbert

Baranczak, Stanislaw. *A Fugitive from Utopia: The Poetry of Zbigniew Herbert*. Cambridge: Harvard University Press, 1987.

Herbert, Zbigniew. *Barbarian in the Garden*. Translated by Michael March and Jaroslaw Anders. Manchester: Carcanet Press, 1985.

——. *The Collected Poems, 1956–1998*. Translated by Alissa Valles, Czeslaw Milosz, and Peter Dale Scott. New York: Ecco Press, 2007.

——. *Elegy for the Departure and Other Poems*. Translated by John Carpenter and Bogdana Carpenter. Hopewell: Ecco Press, 1999.

——. *The King of the Ants: Mythological Essays*. Translated by John Carpenter and Bogdana Carpenter. Hopewell: Ecco Press, 1999.

——. *The Labyrinth on the Sea: Essays*. Translated by John Carpenter and Bogdana Carpenter. New York: Ecco Press, 2005.

——. *Mr. Cogito*. Translated by John Carpenter and Bogdana Carpenter. Oxford, New York: Oxford University Press, 1993.

——. *Report from the Besieged City and Other Poems*. Translated by John Carpenter and Bogdana Carpenter. New York: Ecco Press, 1985.

——. *Selected Poems*. Translated by John Carpenter and Bogdana Carpenter. Oxford, New York: Oxford University Press, 1977.

——. *Selected Poems*. Translated by Czeslaw Milosz and Peter Dale Scott. New York: Ecco Press, 1986.

——. *Still Life with a Bridle: Essays and Apocryphas*. Translated by John Carpenter and Bogdana Carpenter. New York: Ecco Press, 1991.

Kraszewski, Charles S. *Essays on the Dramatic Works of Polish Poet Zbigniew Herbert*. Lewiston, Maine: Edwin Mellen Press, 2002.

Shallcross, Bozena. *Through the Poet's Eye: The Travels of Zagajewski, Herbert, and Brodsky*. Evanston: Northwestern University Press, 2002.

Wislawa Szymborska

Szymborska, Wislawa. *Miracle Fair: Selected Poems of Wislawa Szymborska*. Translated by Joanna Trzeciak. New York: W. W. Norton, 2001.

———. *Monologue of a Dog: New Poems*. Translated by Clare Cavanagh and Stanislaw Baranczak. Orlando: Harcourt, 2006.

———. *Nonrequired Reading: Prose Pieces*. Translated by Clare Cavanagh. New York: Harcourt, 2002.

———. *People on a Bridge: Poems*. Translated by Adam Czerniawski. London, Boston: Forrest Books, 1990.

———. *Poems, New and Collected, 1957–1997*. Translated by Stanislaw Baranczak and Clare Cavanagh. New York: Harcourt, 1998.

———. *Sounds, Feelings, Thoughts: Seventy Poems*. Translated by Magnus Krynski and Robert A. Maguire. Princeton: Princeton University Press, 1981.

———. *View with a Grain of Sand: Selected Poems*. Translated by Stanislaw Baranczak and Clare Cavanagh. New York: Harcourt, 1995.

Wislawa Szymborska: A Stockholm Conference: May 23–24, 2003. Edited by Leonard Neuger and Rikard Wennerholm. Stockholm: Kungl. Vitterhets historie och antikitets, 2006.

Gustaw Herling-Grudzinski

Herling-Grudzinski, Gustaw. *The Island: Three Tales*. Translated by Ronald Strom. New York: Viking, 1993.

———. *The Noonday Cemetery and Other Stories*. Translated by Bill Johnston. New York: New Directions, 2003.

———. *Volcano and Miracle: A Selection of Fiction and Nonfiction from The Journal Written at Night*. Translated by Ronald Strom. New York: Viking, 1996

———. *A World Apart*. Translated by Andrzej Ciozkosz. c.1951. Reprint New York: Arbor House, 1986.

Tadeusz Konwicki

Konwicki, Tadeusz. *The Anthropos-Spectre-Beast*. Translated by George Korwin-Rodziszewski and Audrey Korwin-Rodziszewski. New York: S. Phillips, 1977.

———. *Bohin Manor.* Translated by Richard Lourie. New York: Farrar, Straus and Giroux, 1990.

———. *A Dreambook for Our Time.* Translated by David Welsh. New York: Penguin Books, 1983.

———. *A Minor Apocalypse.* Translated by Richard Lourie. New York: Farrar, Straus and Giroux, 1983.

———. *Moonrise, Moonset.* Translated by Richard Lourie. New York: Farrar, Straus and Giroux, 1987.

———. *New World Avenue and Vicinity.* Translated by Walter Arndt. New York: Farrar, Straus and Giroux, 1991.

———. *The Polish Complex.* Translated by Richard Lourie. New York: Farrar, Straus and Giroux, 1982.

Zechenter, Katarzyna Anna. *The Fiction of Tadeusz Konwicki: Coming to Terms with Post-War Polish History and Politics.* Lewinston, Maine: Edwin Mellen Press, 2007.

Adam Zagajewski

Shallcross, Bozena. *Through the Poet's Eye: The Travels of Zagajewski, Herbert, and Brodsky.* Evanston: Northwestern University Press, 2002.

Zagajewski, Adam. *Another Beauty.* Translated by Clare Cavanagh. New York: Farrar, Straus and Giroux, 2000.

———. *Canvas.* Translated by Renata Gorczynski, Benjamin Ivry, and C. K. Williams. New York: Farrar, Straus and Giroux, 1991.

———. *A Defense of Ardor.* Translated by Clare Cavanagh. New York: Farrar, Straus and Giroux, 2004.

———. *Mysticism for Beginners.* Translated by Clare Cavanagh. New York: Farrar, Straus and Giroux, 1997.

———. *Selected Poems.* Translated by Clare Cavanagh. London: Faber and Faber, 2004.

———. *Solidarity, Solitude: Essays.* Translated by Lillian Vallee. New York: Ecco Press, 1990.

———. *Tremor: Selected Poems*. Translated by Renata Gorczynski. New York: Farrar, Straus and Giroux, 1985.

———. *Two Cities: On Exile, History, and the Imagination*. Translated by Lillian Vallee. New York: Farrar, Straus and Giroux, 1995.

———. *Without End: New and Selected Poems*. Translated by Clare Cavanagh, and Renata Gorczynski, Benjamin Ivry, and C. K. Williams. New York: Farrar, Straus and Giroux, 2002.

INDEX OF NAMES

Milton Keynes UK
Ingram Content Group UK Ltd.
UKHW031850061124
450785UK00004B/101